Praise for *No Point B*

"Change isn't a threat. It's an opportunity. A chance to exercise our moral imagination and move beyond spin and the status quo to do work we're proud of. Caleb Gardner is here to help us see that better is possible."
—Seth Godin, author, *The Practice*

"Navigating change is not merely a skill—it's an organizational superpower. In *No Point B*, Caleb Gardner shows us how it works, and delivers the tools we need to help our own groups thrive in today's world."
—Daniel Coyle, author of *The Culture Code*

"Today more than ever, we need a connoisseur on digital thought leadership to help build meaningful lasting relationships. Caleb Gardner is that connoisseur, and I can't wait for readers to discover his approaches for 21st century change leadership."
—Nathalie Molina Niño, Cofounder & Managing Director at Known Holdings, and author of *Leapfrog: The New Revolution for Women Entrepreneurs*

"Caleb Gardner is at the very top of my list of experts to teach about change leadership in the digital age. Not only was he at the heart of the most dynamic and successful community movement in modern political history, he is also deeply thoughtful, principled, and pragmatic."
—Pamela Slim, business coach, author of *The Widest Net,* and Cofounder of the Main Street Learning Lab in Mesa, Arizona

"Optimism is the cornerstone for creating the change we seek and Caleb has always inspired us with his hopeful approach. Today, with *No Point B*, he delivers a new—and essential—tool for us all to create meaningful change in this fast-paced, ever-evolving world."
—Sarah Kauss, Founder of S'well

"A vital and engaging recipe for embracing change, instead of fighting against it. Recommended for all business leaders!"
—Jay Baer, author of *Youtility: Why Smart Marketing Is About Help, Not Hype*

"Caleb Gardner blends lessons from old truths, new technologies, and his remarkable experience and skill to develop a playbook for social change. He shows the moves to make—and the pitfalls to avoid—as you and your allies nurse a nascent idea from a conversation among two people, to growing a community of supporters and advocates, to a national social movement."
—Robert Sutton, Stanford professor and author of *The No Asshole Rule: Building a Civilized Workplace and Surviving One That Isn't*

"In our technology-accelerated era, change can happen faster than ever—but leading that change responsibly requires a new way of thinking and working. Caleb offers mission-critical guidance for those who want to build something better."

—Kate O'Neil, author of *A Future So Bright* and *Tech Humanist*, CEO of KO Insights, host of *The Tech Humanist Show*

"Caleb Gardner is a big thinker with even bigger ideas about how business can more successfully navigate change. In an era that requires executives to sincerely embrace socially conscious leadership, this book is a must read. *No Point B* is both a reckoning and a road map."

—Joe Mull, author of *Cure for the Common Leader* and *No More Team Drama* and host of the popular *Boss Better Now* podcast

"Every day we hear about new ways our democracy seems to be failing us in the digital realm, but we can't wait for tech companies or the government to fix it. We've got to do it ourselves. Caleb's ideas for how to do that aren't just theoretical—they're urgent. And Caleb's been there; he's walked the walk. We should listen to him."

—Ethan Todras-Whitehill, Cofounder & Executive Director, Swing Left

"What a different world this would be if everyone had read *No Point B* by Caleb Gardner. Imagine always being ready, prepared, and proactively engaged when things change . . . and change they do. If you've grappled with resilience, or if you've found yourself questioning what to do when everything seems upside down, don't panic! Caleb is here. As *No Point B* clearly points out, you don't need to worry about disruption when you can best define the kind of disruption you want . . . and how you strive while surfing through it. Your point A is to read *No Point B*."

—Mitch Joel, author of *Six Pixels of Separation* and *Ctrl Alt Delete*

"Caleb Gardner's *No Point B* is the best playbook I've read for ethical and inclusive political, business, and community leaders who wish to master change as a core competency in a hyper-connected and increasingly complex and volatile world."

—Laura Gassner Otting, *Washington Post* bestselling author of *Limitless*

NO POINT B

Rules for Leading Change in the New Hyper-Connected, Radically Conscious Economy

B

CALEB GARDNER

Matt Holt Books
An Imprint of BenBella Books, Inc.
Dallas, TX

Matt Holt is an imprint of BenBella Books, Inc.
10440 N. Central Expressway
Suite 800
Dallas, TX 75231
benbellabooks.com
Send feedback to feedback@benbellabooks.com

BenBella and *Matt Holt* are federally registered trademarks.

Printed in the United States of America
10 9 8 7 6 5 4 3 2 1

Library of Congress Control Number: 2021062759
ISBN 9781637740996 (hardcover)
ISBN 9781637741009 (electronic)

Editing by Katie Dickman
Copyediting by Ruth Strother
Proofreading by Lisa Story and Denise Pangia
Indexing by WordCo Indexing Services, Inc.
Text design and composition by PerfecType, Nashville, TN
Cover design by Brigid Pearson
Cover image © Shutterstock / Yurchanka Siarhei
Printed by Lake Book Manufacturing

For Caroline, who is stubbornly steadfast and supportive no matter what change comes our way

CONTENTS

What Kind of Disruption Do We Want?

My thoughts about change significantly shifted on a bright day on the South Lawn of the White House in October 2016. The day was sunny, a visual representation of the optimism of the thousands of people arriving for South by South Lawn (SXSL), a White House event inspired by South by Southwest (SXSW), the annual technology and cultural festival held in Austin, Texas, every spring. Called a festival of ideas, art, and action, SXSL was meant to be a cornerstone of an idea President Barack Obama had planted earlier that year at SXSW: the entrepreneurship and creativity shown by American technology companies in the past decade had to be harnessed to solve our toughest challenges as a society, not just to enrich a few billionaires. The event was a celebration of public-private cooperation, and it featured panels with titles such as "Fixing Real Problems" and "How We Make Change" led by activists, actors, and tech entrepreneurs. The late Congressman John Lewis introduced the latter with a call to action to young people: "It is time for each of you as young leaders to get in trouble—good trouble. Get in the way and make some noise. You have the ability. You have the capacity to do it. Just do it."

I wandered the South Lawn that day in awe of the talent present, of the cheery expectations of all involved that we would eventually make progress on the most pressing issues we were facing, such as hunger, climate change, and democratic participation. It was a great moment to reconnect with friends who had worked at the White House, as well as other tech influencers I knew, and share our mutual enthusiasm for what the creative process could achieve to make our world better. But in the back of my mind were concerns I had recently expressed to friends in the industry about technology's effect—especially that of the increasingly toxic social media environment—on the upcoming presidential election. As someone who up until a few weeks prior had run a big part of President Obama's digital platform, I had a stake in believing in the positive influence of tech upon our democracy. That belief had started to wane, but seeing so much talent in one place dedicated to making change made me hopeful again.

We know now, of course, that SXSL wasn't a jumping-off point at all but the apex of an optimism about technology's influence on society that would soon take a dark turn. Already, Facebook was denying its influence upon the 2016 election, refusing to take responsibility for the social engineering of which its platform was capable. Emails provided by Russian hackers were being dumped by WikiLeaks to manipulate news cycles. Conspiracy theories, always prevalent in corners of American life, had found a new home out in the open on the internet, where the paranoid could network with each other and reinforce their own beliefs. The relentless march of technological progress, once thought to be a democratizing force because of the nature of its ability to redistribute power, exposed its dark underbelly and made us aware of its ability to be antidemocratic. Fixing real problems with moral leadership was about to become urgent even as society splintered into factions regarding the role of technology, business, and government in solving those problems.

As SXSL came to an end, my friends and I spread out blankets on the lawn under a cool sky and listened to President Obama in conversation with Dr. Katharine Hayhoe and Leonardo DiCaprio about climate change as the sun set on a one-of-a-kind event from a one-of-a-kind administration. "If we tap the brakes now, then we don't go over the cliff," Obama said. "All of which is to say that as hard as it is for us to start acting now to solve a problem that has not fully manifested itself yet, this is going to be a really important test for humanity and our political system." The Change President wanted us to know that we could still do hard things; that large-scale change was still possible and still up to us.

———

How hard is it to do the right thing?

We're living in an unprecedented time for moral leadership, with the internet creating a rising demand for social awareness and an army of social commentators. But even as the economy becomes radically conscious, the politicization of every issue is making leading by principle increasingly difficult for those wanting to do more than just make a profit. No matter their bent on the political spectrum, business leaders are being forced to choose sides on all kinds of issues. Neutrality as an option is fading as consumers—and often employees and shareholders—demand answers to social issues from company leadership. If there is an Overton window for what we have considered acceptable business conversation, similar to the range of what we have considered mainstream political conversation, it is shifting as the internet breaks down silos between our personal and professional lives.

Not only does it feel more imperative than ever to run a socially conscious company—and to live a socially conscious life—but the need to communicate about that imperative, to morally perform in the global social media theater, also seems increasingly paramount in an environment where not communicating might as well mean not existing. Because we've been given the most powerful digital megaphones in history in the form of our personal devices, a decision not to use those megaphones to speak out about an issue can be seen as a vote for the status quo. The new digital media environment has created a new kind of moral hazard for company leaders, who now have to battle with perception and reputation on a thousand fronts.

But actual moral leadership, not just communicating well about social issues, remains difficult—I believe more difficult than we as consumers understand. The complexity of trying to operate at the intersection of business and social good is illustrated by how many separate conversations are happening with many different frameworks: organizing structures like B Corporations and L3Cs (low-profit limited liability companies); accounting and financial frameworks like triple bottom line and ESG (environmental, social, and governance); and networks like Conscious Capitalism and Kindred. The environment has become rich with perspectives about why we should run a conscious company and is increasingly flooded with models for how to measure a company's commitment to social good. But left out of this conversation is an acknowledgment that the transition from the status quo to better is actually extremely difficult.

As business gets pulled into politics, complicated issues get painted as black and white because our ideologies don't allow much room for gray. But businesses operate in complex environments, with every decision creating cascading effects both for the companies' profitability and the communities in which the companies operate. We expect company leaders to operate with perfect moral clarity and are quick to call them out when we believe they are making decisions for the sake of profit alone. But I know from experience that executives often want to do the right thing and are frequently faced with a lack of clarity on what the right thing may be in a particular situation. Leadership requires moral imagination and intentionality, and for certain types of companies, leadership comes with a lot of historical baggage in the form of moral and technical debt, liabilities built up over time based on how those companies have chosen to operate since their founding.

Traditional change management models don't acknowledge the speed and complexity of operating in a digital world. They focus on one linear, often highly technical initiative at a time rather than on providing tools across multiple horizons to tackle cascading effects and impending disruptions. They also don't provide for the kind of philosophical underpinning needed to move in a more ethical direction as a company. The hyper-moralized media environment in which we operate doesn't allow for making mistakes without an avalanche of negative attention—meaning companies have to master not only operating more ethically, but also communicating more aggressively about the kinds of changes they're making as well as acknowledging and responding to mistakes more quickly. If we're truly going to move the global economy in a more ethical and inclusive direction, we need new rules for how we change, and more leaders need to master adaptive change as a core competency.

I've always been fascinated by change—how we as individuals make brave choices to go in new directions as well as how society evolves over time and institutions change in response. (I even have a tattoo of a delta, the mathematical symbol for change, on my arm.) After majoring in history as an undergraduate and eventually going back to school for my MBA, I became fascinated with the historical dissonance the internet was creating between old power structures and new media. I especially felt that social media presented an opportunity for corporations, nongovernmental organizations (NGOs), and governments to hear directly from their people about what they wanted. Throughout my career working for global consulting firms, communications agencies, startups, and nonprofits, and as a political organizer for President Barack Obama, that dissonance continued to force change in all areas of society—not always for the better—even as old institutions dragged their bureaucratic feet. To this day, coming out of a once-in-a-lifetime global pandemic and massive social upheaval, most institutional leaders still continue to be blind to the massive disruptions ahead of them and the urgency of changing in kind.

My career has been at the intersection of digital disruption, social activism, and the future of work. Having been in rooms with both CEOs and political activists over the last decade, I've become increasingly fascinated with the idea of a socially conscious business, one that tries to operate in a complex and connected world with some degree of ethical decision-making. Many C-suite leaders have this ambition. Of course they care about revenue, and in an environment of increased digital competition they often have to watch their defensive flank to even survive. But many harbor the ambition of doing well by doing good and understand that to do so means better consumer relationships, happier employees, and, increasingly, happier shareholders. And their pay is more often being linked to new socially conscious criteria like ESG goals whether they want them to be or not. Complexity and political risk present real barriers to that ambition. The massive amount of effort it takes to turn a global corporation, often originally built using labor or environmental exploitation, into a net good for society requires multiple investments across multiple horizons. And it comes with a downside: to speak an ethical ambition into the air is to invite criticism of all the ways you're not meeting that ambition.

But I believe aiming for better still has less risk than its opposite. Business expectations are shifting quickly, and those who believe they can still operate in a professional environment while ignoring the larger needs of society will quickly find that their customers and employees think otherwise. The shareholder primacy era of defining business success is coming to an end. In 2019, 181

CEOs of major corporations signed the Business Roundtable's updated "Statement on the Purpose of a Corporation":

> Since 1978, Business Roundtable has periodically issued Principles of Corporate Governance that include language on the purpose of a corporation. Each version of that document issued since 1997 has stated that corporations exist principally to serve their shareholders. It has become clear that this language on corporate purpose does not accurately describe the ways in which we and our fellow CEOs endeavor every day to create value for all our stakeholders, whose long-term interests are inseparable.

The statement goes on to include investments in labor, ethical supply chains, and community support as equally important to customer and shareholder value. There's no question that business leaders are moving in more ethical and inclusive directions. The question is how they are going to get there from where they are now.

This book is my attempt at outlining what I believe are core concepts for leading change in the kind of world we live in now, one that is hyper-connected, complex, and politically volatile. If our business models are moving from shareholder primacy to stakeholder inclusion, we can't expect the same models of change management, leadership, and innovation to get us to where we need to go next. We have to understand the new digital imperatives for communication and how the internet creates the reality we live in. We have to understand what is real and what is overinflated about the political risks of that so-called reality, and how to navigate changing our minds while living in the public eye. And we have to get a grip on how we bring our employees along with change that is going to be complex, how we constantly persuade them we're moving in the right direction even as the right direction may shift.

Each chapter begins with deconstructing how the major trends discussed affect our behavior as individuals before going on to talk about how these individual behaviors have created new rules for understanding an organization's ability to change. This is intentional for several reasons. Understanding organizational behavior through the lens of complexity thinking and systems analysis means we have to examine the individual components of a system even as we examine how the sum of its parts creates a system in motion. But more specifically, I believe the internet has turned us into a society of individual actors, especially in the US, where we'd already embraced rugged individualism with a religious fervor. Our personal devices encapsulate our news, our work, our entertainment, and, importantly, our social circles. Reality itself is now filtered through our personal preferences, and anyone seeking to do organizational change can't ignore the reality-forming influence of our connected lives.

This kind of change management has no end point. The journey to becoming a better version of our companies, our societies, ourselves is one that is never-ending. There are always new disruptions, new information to consider, and new critiques of our ways of working that we have to evaluate. Then once we know better, we have to figure out how to be better again. The work of constant adaptation is exhausting even outside ethical concerns, and throwing in the emotional weight of engaging in social issues creates a seemingly paralyzing mix of factors that stops many leaders from engaging in this work at all. But we don't have a choice. The new radically conscious economy is moving forward, with or without us, outlining new parameters for competitive advantage and acceptable corporate behavior.

I've always felt that separating the concept of economic disruption from its ethical implications was a mistake (market disruption is, after all, a displacement of jobs and consumer choices), but often business leaders talk about disruption as a net good in and of itself. Partly this is due to America's worship of innovators, but it's also because of the notion of the inevitability of technological progress and our obsession with those able to forecast where it's going. If I've learned anything since SXSL, it's that framing progress as inevitable leads us to a fatalistic view of the economy, when in fact the direction of the economy is up to us. Call it the pragmatic optimism of a former political organizer, but I believe we will only get the kind of disruption we are willing to fight for.

1

There Is No Point B

I remember being struck by the venerableness of the first corporate campus I visited. The sprawling nature of its dedicated buildings—marketing here, R&D there, and so on—stood as physical representation of both long-term success and a will for power, like a corporate Stonehenge. I visited many Fortune 500 corporate headquarters in the late aughts with teams from Edelman, a global public relations firm, as part of various pitches and presentations. As a young digital strategist, I was meant to represent the new wave of internet communications, especially social media, that the firm saw as its future.

One pitch in particular stands out to me now. I was looking out of a large interior window at a view of a corporate cityscape in a building several stories high with a circular design meant to collapse people and ideas serendipitously in on themselves. Our team was waiting for a chief marketing officer (CMO) and several brand managers from this particular consumer goods company in the main executive conference room. The room was meant to communicate importance due to its size and building positioning (hence the window). And stories about the company's past were documented on the walls of the exterior hallway, so one couldn't help but run into its history on the way into the room. It was my second, maybe third pitch, so I was nervous, running over my notes while gazing at the corporate denizens busy with their particular cogs. I was there to be an ambassador for the future, and I remember feeling the weight of history, wondering how many of the people I was watching would have their jobs upended in the next decade or two, or even in the next year or two.

Eventually, the CMO and her team arrived, and the usual pleasantries were exchanged. I remember how she commanded the room like a queen holding court, all eyes on her to determine whether she favored the entertainment of the day or not. We launched into our presentation, which followed a formulaic cadence we'd been preaching to several clients: communications is changing, and you need to evolve; your brand is no longer owned by you but exists in the push-and-pull of thousands of online ambassadors and detractors who experience your products. When it was my turn to speak, I tried my best to lend authority to our theories with data points about the rise of social media platforms. Twitter was around four years old, YouTube was five, and Facebook was already more than six years into completely restructuring our social landscape as we knew it. Now was the time to act boldly, recognize the disruptive power of digital, and shift budgets accordingly.

The CMO nodded along with our presentation, listening respectfully, and she and the brand managers asked thoughtful questions along the way about elements of our proposed program. At the end, all eyes turned toward her for a final assessment.

"I really like this," she said. "And I thank you for bringing us such innovative ideas. But ultimately, it's too risky for us. We know what works—we've got data to show it. I just don't feel comfortable significantly shifting our money away from things that have proven their value over time to something like Facebook, which is only a few years old. What if social media turns out to be a fad?"

As we walked out that day, leaving corporate Stonehenge behind, I was struck for the first time by the power of collective momentum to propel such a respected corporation in a particular, well-worn direction. Ultimately, our team got approved for a smaller, less ambitious program that let a few of the company's brands dip their toes into the waters of digital marketing. We were happy to even get our foot in the door.

Several years and several CMOs later, the company finally got serious about shifting its spend to digital, but not before several of its brands were disrupted by new direct-to-consumer businesses that were digitally native, and the company's stock price took a significant hit. The once dominant conglomerate found itself struggling for relevancy. It wasn't the only one. The fated decision to delay taking digital seriously as both a potentially disruptive force and a massive opportunity was one we saw play out repeatedly in those early days of what came to be called Web 2.0, the rise of participatory media online that would change not only how corporations approached their consumer bases, but also how society functions as we know it. By the time we were having those key conversations with CMOs across the world, the signs of social media's rise as a dominant force were there. So why were so many so bad at understanding what was about to happen?

Remembering the Past & Predicting the Future

As it turns out, we're bad at predicting the future and terrible at understanding the past. This warps our understanding of what's coming and the possible implications of change.

According to the psychologist Daniel Gilbert, who has extensively studied a phenomenon known as the end-of-history illusion, human beings are works in progress who believe we're finished. We consistently look to our past and find evidence of how we've grown, how our opinions and perceptions have evolved over time as we've matured, but we underestimate our capacity to continue to grow in the future. We believe this version of ourselves is pretty much the final version and that we'll think, act, and feel the same in the future as we do now, leading us to make decisions that satisfy short-term desires rather than long-term goals. We rarely give our future selves appropriate empathy.

The hindsight bias we apply to our perception of the predictability of past events (which, in retrospect, *obviously* had to turn out the way they did) gets amplified when those past events affected us directly because we hook our own past events into preexisting context. We put our memories in a box of our own understanding, which is why new experiences with no connections to other events are harder to maintain in our brains.

I remember Gabi, a woman I saw at a recent conference, because we used to work together and she told me a story about how she was treated by Nate, our former coworker. I don't remember what's-his-name, someone I met at the same conference, because he created a startup in an industry about which I know nothing. Our memories are selective in this way. The narrative we tell ourselves about the past is never fully representative of reality.

Memories are more malleable than we realize. In fact, our memories evolve over time as we add more context and experiences to our lives. If past events now seem to be inevitable, it's because the context we have now allows us to reexamine them with fresh eyes. Gabi's story about Nate's behavior hits differently in the context of #MeToo than it might have before, when I was less educated about the harassment women experience in the workplace. In this way we use creative thinking on the past and are constantly retelling our own stories to ourselves.

We use the same parts of our brain to imagine the past as we do to imagine the future, and this is where our own experiences limit our ability to predict what will happen. Our emotions about the past cloud our ability to forecast and make it impossible for us to be impartial observers. Important psychological concepts to behavioral economics like *salience*, *availability*, and *accessibility* are all fancy ways of saying we give more weight to events with greater emotional resonance, especially if they've happened to us personally and even more so if they've happened to us recently. Therefore we may fear dying in a plane crash because we just read about a downed aircraft, or fear getting injured in a car crash because of a recent fender bender, but give no prominence to catching a disease from a global pandemic, a once-in-a-generation event for which we have no context, even though the latter is by far more likely.

The malleability of our memories and the extent to which we underestimate their effect on our perception of reality are important in the context of trying to understand and manage change. We see change as an external force we have to react to accordingly, but, whether we realize it or not, our experiences with change actually change us. Our identity is in constant dialogue with the circumstances of our lives, with our input of information. We change in spite of ourselves, but the direction a transformation takes—whether it is constructive or destructive to our overall health, to our companies or communities, or to society at large—depends upon the inputs we receive and the intentionality with which we interpret them. Identity change is inevitable; we grow only when we point that change in a specific direction.

Most of us have a hard time rationally looking at a set of data points and understanding their implications without making counterfactual arguments to ourselves about possible outcomes that are self-serving. Social scientists call this phenomenon unrealistic optimism: a cognitive bias that causes us to believe we are less likely to experience a negative event even in the face of evidence. Disaster preparedness advocates have known this for decades.

In a *TIME* magazine poll conducted in 2006, with Hurricane Katrina fresh in the American consciousness, about half of respondents said they had personally experienced a natural disaster or emergency situation—but only 16 percent said they were "very well prepared" for the next one. For those not prepared, about half explained their lack of preparedness by saying they don't live in a high-risk area, even though 91 percent of Americans live in places with a moderate to high risk of disasters such as earthquakes, tornadoes, or wildfires.

We constantly confuse the challenge of picturing the future with the probability that any given future could happen to us. It's why so few of us saw COVID-19 coming. Even most of the experts missed the implications of the novel coronavirus coming out of Wuhan, China, toward the end of 2019. As late as February 29, 2020, well after China publicly admitted the virus was being spread person-to-person and weeks after the first US COVID-related death, Dr. Anthony Fauci, in whose glow of expertise and responsibility many of us basked during the pandemic, was still saying, "You don't need to change anything you're doing"—even as he warned that the situation could change quickly. Experts try to make predictions work within similar mental paradigms as the rest of us, but they often do it in groups. By February 2020, the scientific community had not yet reached a consensus on the right response to the coronavirus.

Most of the time, so-called experts in many fields face very little accountability for their forecasting. Op-ed political pundits, sports talking heads, stock market analysts, and others face few consequences for getting it wrong but can often be hailed as geniuses when their predictions come true. Few face any kind of "clairvoyance test" that professional forecasters could use to determine accuracy. Philip Tetlock, Annenberg University professor at the University of Pennsylvania, has studied the science of forecasting for more than forty years, and he has shown that those in the prediction business are notoriously bad at getting it right. In his 2005 book, *Expert Political Judgment*, he compared experts' predictions unfavorably to monkeys throwing darts at a dartboard. What makes them so often wrong? Besides a general lack of accountability in their fields for bad forecasts, many experts suffer from systematic overconfidence that leads them to rarely change their mind quickly in response to new evidence. Tetlock calls it dogmatism: the tendency to use high IQs to create increasingly complex justifications for one's preferred prediction rather than reasons to oppose it.

Data Isn't Magic

Don't we have enough data available now that we don't need to rely on subject matter experts to know what the future holds? Can't we rely on impartial analysis of the right kinds of data to tell us with some level of certainty what might happen? Sort of. As someone who ran one of the largest digital programs in the world, I have come face-to-face with the limits of what so-called big data can provide.

Take for example a study produced by Rutgers University and the tech companies Foursquare and SocialFlow after Hurricane Sandy ravaged the New York City area in 2012. More than 20 million tweets about the storm were generated between October 27 and November 1. The study combined that data with Foursquare location data to show consumer habits before and after the storm, such as when grocery shopping peaked and when nightlife picked up after the storm. On its surface this data seemed significant, but as Dr. Kate Crawford, a leading scholar for AI and big data, pointed out at the time, most of the data came from Manhattan rather than more severely affected locations around the city, where extended blackouts and restricted cellular access limited smartphone use. The application of big data is tricky in this way: technologies are always adopted at different paces in different communities, and the interpretation of data at scale needs social context as much as statistical analysis.

The private sector preaches about data with a religious fervor—tech industry leaders treat it as a sort of unsulliable holy text upon which their faith in progress is built—but for all the advances in artificial intelligence, machine learning, and other biblical-technical beasts that have come to dominate modern life, the truth is that there are still too many variables, too many pieces of the puzzle emerging on any given day, for any computer to truly comprehend the world, much less the rational-irrational dialectic of the human mind.

Many companies have used predictive analytics in ways that confound the modern imagination, such as Amazon's ability to anticipate the buying patterns of its customers and ensure the promise of Amazon Prime's shipping windows. But those predictions are based on more limited data sets and are aimed at answering more specific questions, such as what consumers will want to buy next. The ability to truly anticipate the kind of human behavior that may influence customer purchasing patterns over long periods of time—or, more specifically, the ability to distinguish what is relevant from what is irrelevant, from weather patterns to breakups to unanticipated pandemics—requires a substantial amount of relevant data. And that assumes that we buy into the narrative of impartial data analysis done by impartial software in the first place.

Many modern critiques of algorithms, including those with some of the most significant influence over our lives such as the

Facebook News Feed and Google search engine, are focused on the implicit biases of their designers. Technology isn't neutral; it is colored by the humans who create it. And algorithms learn by being fed data sets that also display bias, such as crime statistics that inform deploying police resources predominantly in communities of color.

Technology as Anticipation

Recent history is rife with leaders, even leaders in technology, who dramatically underestimate technology's impact. Thomas Watson, president of IBM in 1943, famously said, "I think there is a world market for maybe five computers." Robert Metcalfe, founder of 3Com, wrote in 1995 that "the Internet will soon go spectacularly supernova and in 1996 catastrophically collapse." And in 2007, Steve Ballmer, the then CEO of Microsoft, said in an interview with *USA Today*, "There's no chance that the iPhone is going to get any significant market share." Most of us are terrible at seeing beyond our own self-interest to predict the future.

Technology is all about anticipation: the industry thrives on what's new and what's next, and not just from the standpoint of selling us the future as consumers. Many who work in tech industries are passionate believers in the future for the future's sake. They believe that better technology is a good in and of itself, bringing with it a better understanding of the world and more control over it. They also believe the pace of change is inevitable. A prediction made in 1975 by the cofounder of Intel, Gordon Moore, has since become known as Moore's Law because of its prescience. Moore predicted that the number of transistors in an integrated circuit, the backbone of computing power, would double about every two years. As society has increasingly focused on the tech that enables our everyday lives, this future orientation has seeped into our consciousness, creating a massive distortion of our present and a warping of our sense of time. There's always the next thing.

Our expectation for every new invention, every iteration of our favorite gadget, every new hype that is going to change everything—blockchain, 5G, wearables, augmented and virtual reality, direct-to-consumer, autonomous vehicles, artificial intelligence, Internet of Things, micromobility—creates a dissonance between our present and future realities in a way that never lets us fully appreciate how transformative the past few decades have actually been.

If you've ever traveled for a vacation, you've probably experienced a phenomenon psychologists call the return trip effect, the feeling that the trip to the destination took much longer than the trip back. No one's quite sure why we experience time in this way, but one theory is that our brains keep track of time in two separate systems: one that attempts to mathematically keep track of the passage of time, and one in which we tell stories to ourselves about previous events and how long they took. The centrality of technology's place in our society, and its cascading anticipatory nature, is creating this phenomenon on a massive scale.

Consistently awaiting the next big thing actually skews our sense of when it will arrive and how disruptive it will be when it gets here. It's the reason for the famous Gartner Hype Cycle, which shows how a technology will reach a peak of inflated expectations only to deflate to a trough of disillusionment long before its value and broad market applicability becomes apparent.

The effect is that we don't realize the power we've been given in such a short amount of time. The iPhone was introduced just fifteen years ago as of this writing, and as we approach the tipping point of more than half the world owning smartphones, we rarely stop to examine how much power that has given us as individuals living in a global community. We carry around in our pockets the world's information and access to some of the most powerful communications platforms ever invented, on some of the smartest computers ever invented, capable of documenting every facet of our lives. In the context of history, we've all become Peter Parkers practically overnight, with the powers of Spider-Man, but no Uncle Ben whispering into our ears, asking us how we're going to use those powers responsibly.

Change Won't Stop Coming

I majored in history as an undergrad, partially because I briefly entertained the idea of going to law school, and partially because I've always been fascinated by big trends in humanity and the stories we tell ourselves about the past. So I don't consider it a complete non sequitur that most of my career has been about digital transformation: the effects of rapidly advancing technology on people's identities and social networks, the implications for the way work is done, the overtones of purpose and power that are changing systems of self-governance like democracy—and, we now know, enabling leaders with authoritarian tendencies to bypass traditional media criticism. What has been consistently frustrating to me when I talk with business leaders and politicians about these big shifts is how obsessed we are about the future without giving ourselves the capacity to deal with the change that is already here. History is full of events that are disruptive not because no one saw them coming, but because of how entrenched routines and mindsets had become.

In his 1970 work *Future Shock*, futurist Alvin Toffler, watching the dawn of the Information Age, predicted that the accelerating rate of technological and social change society was experiencing would be so overwhelming that it would leave people disoriented and (ironically, from the standpoint of the twenty-first century) disconnected. Even before the smartphone took its place at the center of how we experience the world, Toffler predicted that information overload would cause enormous social problems.

The concept of future shock may seem forward looking, but it's a term diagnosing our ability to deal with the present and with the future collapsing into what we believe about ourselves now. The accelerating pace of technology has made our present lives feel futuristic even as we struggle to understand these new tools and how to use them. We feel the dissonance of the culture around us not keeping up. The fact is that we are dealing with a cascading series of disruptions, some obvious and some so small they have nearly imperceptible implications, like the very beginning of an exponential set of dominoes. Disruption isn't new: America's famed transcontinental Pony Express lasted just eighteen months before the telegraph completely killed its business model in 1861. But as Toffler predicted, our ability to process the accelerating and interconnected nature of our disruptions has taken a serious hit.

And yet we remain obsessed with the future at the detriment of our capacity to deal with the present. In my career, I've seen many leaders and executives fawning over what's around the corner, what new trend they should watch, what new wave may be the one they can ride into infamy. *What's next?* they have asked, begging for just a little more insight than their peers got. History is full of hero Netflixes and naive Blockbusters, and no one wants to be the latter. But our obsession with what's coming—something we are excessively bad at knowing anyway—often blinds us to our ability to deal with what's right in front of us. If we haven't made ourselves more adaptable, haven't built into our operating model the ability to deal with constant change, what does it matter what's around the corner? We're not ready for it anyway.

Sometimes the future gets thrust upon us even when we see it coming. In June 2021, leadership at the oil giant Exxon Mobil was the victim of an embarrassing loss. A tiny hedge fund called Engine No. 1 was able to successfully install three board directors with the goal of pushing the company on its reduction of carbon emissions. The energy giant had paid lip service to green initiatives for years. In 2020, it announced it was meeting the goals of the global Paris Agreement negotiated during the Obama administration and was aiming for "industry-leading greenhouse gas performance across its businesses by 2030." But Engine No. 1's founder, Chris James, argued that Exxon's management wasn't changing fast enough. The upstart fund was able to win the support of institutional investors such as Vanguard and BlackRock to support its shareholder activism, and Wall Street took notice.

The mistake made by Exxon management was thinking it had time to transition to clean energy on its own schedule, and that the best approach to maintaining both shareholder value and the energy needs of its customers and clients was to move at an intentional pace consistent with its competitors and the global community. Company leadership thought it was very future-focused. But its most important investors thought otherwise. They framed an aggressive approach to reducing climate risk as necessary to protect shareholder value in the long term. For too long Wall Street investors have worried more about quarterly gains than long-term stakeholder value, but the ground is shifting out from underneath companies like Exxon. Some say the future arrives faster than we think; I say the sooner we understand the future as collapsing in on the present, the better positioned we'll be to deal with it.

We have to stop seeing disruption as a series of singular events that we have the ability to head off and look the dirty truth in the face: the influences of disruption are incalculable and impossible to predict, and our reactions to them often come with unintended consequences that create even more confusion. Existing in modern society means constantly pivoting, constantly re-evaluating our position, or getting lost in the infinite possibilities of a changing world. We have been taught to see change as a linear process we go through in reaction to stimuli, when we go from being one thing to being another, better thing. Our ability to deal with an uncertain future means reframing change as a recursive process, one that requires constant repetition and practice. It's not going from point A to point B. In fact, there is no point B.

That doesn't mean we should completely stop thinking about the future, just that we should recognize, as Einstein said, that time and space are modes by which we think, not conditions in which we live. We can admit how bad we are at knowing what's going to happen and still make attempts at prediction with a bit of humility. According to Tetlock, the best forecasters approach the job of the future with a clear understanding of changing data and a fluid intelligence that allows them to process new information as it comes, and are not necessarily those who have subject matter expertise in certain areas. In fact, Tetlock has found that when it comes to making accurate predictions, there are diminishing returns for specialized knowledge, and too much expertise is what leads to overconfidence and the inability to adjust mental models. He uses philosopher Isaiah Berlin's idea of foxes and hedgehogs to draw the contrast: hedgehogs view the world through one big, defining idea, whereas foxes understand the world's complexity, are generally skeptical of any kind of grand framework, and draw from a variety of experiences to make conclusions. As a result, foxes, even those who have studied a field less vigorously than an expert, tend to make better forecasters.

We need more foxes running our companies, our governments, and our communities. If change is something we have to be doing constantly, interpreting small amounts of emerging data, making predictions about the future, and pivoting accordingly has to become a leadership competency. It doesn't mean every prediction will necessitate some big restructure of how business is done, but it does mean that leaders have to be prepared to recognize how little they know about how to do things the right way at any given time. Leadership that is married to one strategy, without the opportunity for critique, will increasingly fail.

The smartest organizations I've worked with think critically about what they don't know about the future and create infrastructure for evaluating emerging data and implementing structural change on an ongoing basis. Recently, 18 Coffees worked with a national nonprofit organization to implement change teams in several local chapters in major markets, local staff dedicated to constant adaptation with modern change management principles.

Importantly, these change teams were not made up of senior leaders, who often have a vision for where the company should go but are too busy with the day-to-day work of managing the business to focus on road-mapping and implementing transformation efforts. Change teams are composed of influencers in the organization, some of whom are close to the frontline work, who can often see the need for business model adaptation before the CEO does, and who own the success of the change because it directly affects their work. But the most important part of the change teams is their consistent dedication to adaptation: the teams aren't focused on one specific initiative but rather have a constant eye on where the organization is and where it needs to go.

This kind of consistent dedication is the only way not to become overwhelmed with future shock. We need mechanisms outside of our day-to-day work that constantly force us to look at what we're doing with fresh eyes, and leaders who are able to see beyond their current priorities. This often means making investments on multiple horizons. I've counseled clients to use the 70/20/10 rule: 70 percent of their money and time should go toward defensive maneuvers, optimizing and protecting current lines of business that are working; 20 percent should go toward investments in the immediate future where a reasonable amount of data points have assured us of their worth; and 10 percent should go to big ideas and new innovations that may not work out long term, but the consistent investment will protect against disruption. The time horizons for finding value from all of those investments are different, but all of them are important to invest in now.

Most of our institutions need new leaders capable of not just talking about future-proofing our organizations, but also seeing how the future is collapsing in on us now. The old change management model—unfreeze the organization, change it, and then refreeze it—is insufficient in a world where a new disruption happens before the company can thaw. We have to reframe change not as a linear thing we go through, but as a core competency for surviving in an increasingly uncertain world. From now on, all leadership is change leadership.

Overcoming Anticipatory Anxiety

We've been empowered beyond anything we can comprehend as individuals, we've been given supercomputers we carry around in our pockets that connect us to the global community, but our governments, corporations, global NGOs, and other pillars of our society have barely had time to adapt. With our focus on the future comes a hindsight bias about our societal transformation and its inevitability, and mismatched expectations about how quickly our institutions can keep up. It's hard to reconcile what new technological power should mean for ourselves with how that should change our ideals and values. It's even harder for our businesses, governments, media, and other pillars of modern society, which by their naturally bureaucratic nature have to transform much more slowly, to keep up with such a fast-moving world.

Our expectations as citizens and employees are driven by our experiences as consumers, such as real-time responsiveness, overnight shipping, and having the answers to everything practically at our fingertips. The cultural lag between our expectation of immediacy and the responsiveness of democratic government is especially jarring right now and is throwing the proximity of our social, economic, and environmental crises—and the inadequacy of our public response—into the spotlight. Combine that with the urgency of the issues we're facing, including the increasingly obvious effects of climate change and, as I write this in 2021, a global pandemic, it's no wonder we're frustrated.

In the latest Edelman Trust Barometer, a global survey done every year on trust in institutions by my old employer, there is an incredible 47-point gap between trust in government in the US, where our great deliberative institutions intentionally force a slowing down of action in favor of compromise, and in China, where the government is more able to act forcefully and swiftly in response to problems. There is a similar 35-point gap in the trust in business.

China's ability to seize opportunities in the global market while supporting innovation at home, as well as its ability to have the government and the private sector act as one voice to support national priorities, will continue to make it a force with which to be reckoned on the global stage while the biggest democracies in the world continue to deal with government infighting and antagonism between the public and private sectors. The deliberative bodies of

democracy are in danger precisely because they've been too deliberative, too often partisan, and have misread the urgency of the
moment. We have to figure out a way to set realistic expectations
for our ability to make social progress in a democracy, given how
accustomed we've become to the immediacy of the world. But more
importantly, we have to figure out ways to move more quickly in
response to urgent problems.

Those of us who still believe democracy and democratic participation are the best form of governance have to be a part of helping
our institutions evolve faster. The urgency of the moment depends
on it. Same goes for our workplaces, for the charities to which we
give, for the causes about which we care. It's not enough to only
complain from the sidelines about what's going wrong. Change only
truly happens when those most affected by it get involved in making it happen.

We may be bad at predicting the future, but that doesn't mean
we should be undisturbed in the face of disruption. The challenge
of predicting change isn't the same as the improbability of change.
The fact that the future is still so opaque should make us even more
focused on our ability to change our minds, change our companies,
and change our policy positions quickly in the face of new data.
Technological advances won't stop coming, and our dialogue with
them will continue to change our understanding of how the world
works. Those of us who can stay curious, and (unlike the experts)
admit when we're wrong and pivot accordingly, will have a competitive advantage going forward into the unknowable.

Writing this book in a global pandemic, with the economy in
fits and starts as employees consider whether they'll ever go back

into an office, I'm struck by how much of our lives in the past few years has been defined by waiting. Beyond our preoccupation with evolving technology, the pandemic and the chaotic Trump years were a stress test on expectations of normalcy as we went through a series of milestones designed for maximum anxiety: a presidential election, waiting to go back to the office and back to school, anticipating a vaccine and then anticipating distribution of the vaccine, and waiting to see friends and family again. The year 2020 seemed custom designed to skew our sense of time as each day blurred into another.

All that played out while we were adjusting to a new normal that saw many businesses dramatically shift their ways of working almost overnight. Fear of uncertainty can lead to decision paralysis, and in my career I've seen leaders freeze up at the prospect of an ambiguous future, causing a massive wave of anticipatory anxiety among staff already skittish about change—which leads to the likelihood of heightened organizational defensive routines once a change in direction is finally determined. But recent years have shown how quickly leaders can actually pivot once presented with circumstances that demand dramatic transformation, even without perfect information. The coronavirus pandemic's imperativeness not only created permission for leaders to take action, it also created clarity among staff about why the change had to happen. The internal will to do better, typically a slog for leaders to develop over time, manifested practically overnight.

Therein lies the rub with our skewed sense of time. We are able to move quickly when presented with a pandemic-like situation that calls for action, but dramatic circumstances that call for our attention are always happening underneath the surface. Most disruption happens as a slow burn effect on our ability to operate, a barely perceivable sea change that doesn't disturb how we do business until all at once, it does. Recognizing there's no point B means conducting ourselves with pandemic-level urgency all the time, getting comfortable moving quickly with a certain level of uncertainty while navigating potentially thorny ethical issues caused by the complexity of our operating environments. Imagine if your organization moved with the same level of urgency and clarity it did in 2020 at all times, and you'll begin to understand the operating model this moment calls for.

2

The Internet Makes Change Harder (and Easier)

When I was twelve, a series of strange events occurred, and I got my first computer. And the world changed. But let me back up. For most of my life up to that point, I'd lived in a manufactured home community (trailer park) on the outskirts of a midsize city in Oklahoma with my working-class parents. My mother met my stepfather while scraping by waiting tables after she left my abusive and schizophrenic biological father. I was three, or maybe two, so most of what I know from that time period I've heard secondhand. My biological father and his history had been erased from the family record. And then, seemingly out of nowhere, he bought me my first computer.

Money arrived in the mail along with a note that it was specifically to be used to buy me a computer. My father, I would later learn, had always had entrepreneurial ambition, and he hoped to instill some of that future thinking in me from afar. But it was the early '90s, and personal computers, at least in Oklahoma, were still relatively rare. My parents had no clue where to start, had no technology expertise, and had never desired a PC of their own. So one weekend they shuttled me to a local department store to have the salesman explain our options. Some technology jargon was introduced to us ("How much RAM do you need?" "Would you like a CD-ROM drive?"), and I was asked my opinion. But I knew about as much as my parents did, only having been exposed to the shared computers a few of my classrooms had used for limited projects. But you could play games! That much I knew, and that was about the extent of my intent for my new toy.

We settled on a desktop Packard Bell (a terrible choice in retrospect), and it felt like we'd officially entered the future. I became the envy of my neighborhood friends, who would come over to play *Mortal Kombat*; my cousins, who mostly lived in the more rural parts of Oklahoma, treated the computer like a shrine to civilization. Like some kind of Greek god extending his hand to change the circumstances of his children, my father, the schizophrenic, the absentee—and my mother, who dared to let him influence my life this one time—extended his favor and successfully set his son on a path that would come to be defined by technology, connectivity, and entrepreneurial ambition.

When the internet came to our household, it came in the form of a Christmas gift. Three years after the introduction of the Packard Bell into our household, I was begging my parents to allow it to become more than a giant video game console. At that point, many of my wealthier friends had jacked in, taking their digital exploration to new, envious heights. The closest I had come to that then was starting a semi–pen pal relationship with a few friends via a Juno email account, which required the same two- to three-minute chaotic and cacophonous dial-up process as those with full internet access, only to send one email at a time. I was hungry for more. My parents relented, subscribing to a local internet provider who provided five 3.5-inch floppy disks for installation. My parents wrapped the disks for me and put the gift of the internet underneath the Christmas tree that year.

What followed were teenage years spent exploring new digital frontiers. It was the age of AOL chat rooms and ASL (age, sex, location) inquiries, of GeoCities as the first plug-and-play forms of self-expression. Eventually, Napster made a splash, and we discovered that the internet had the potential to replace things from real life. These were the first inklings of participation in a larger global community, of internet presence being essential to the creation of meaning—and for a rural area like the one in which I grew up, it felt like a revelation. I knew even then that my online presence was an important part of my off-line social circles.

The digital revolution came slowly to Oklahoma. Rural areas like the one we lived in are slower to adopt new technologies than the bigger cities, but not always for reasons of choice. Broadband providers have little incentive to build infrastructure where there aren't very many users. For us, growing up with slow dial-up modems, broadband was like a whisper, a rumor so precious that we didn't dare to hope for it. Rural kids today often rely on the local McDonald's or other public Wi-Fi to find the connectivity they need.

The rural-urban digital divide is only one example of the cultural lag the new digital world represents. As some people become increasingly connected and reliant personally and professionally on being plugged in at all times, others have no hardware and no infrastructure with which to access the global community. As some map out new careers in technology-savvy fields, others are just learning the latest version of Microsoft Word in order to do basic word processing. And while a few are experienced enough media critics to know what's real and what's fake online, plenty of people still have a hard time distinguishing a local blog's opinion from Pulitzer award-winning journalism. I experienced the very beginning of a cultural dissonance caused by the internet and connected devices, and I was lucky to have enough support to plug in and really grasp what was happening to society in ways that were personally and professionally beneficial. But that cultural lag between the internet's potential and society's discernment remains.

I believe the future of the internet is the future of humanity, and if we want to make our organizations better—if we ever want to make anything better—it requires understanding, navigating, and sometimes fixing our connected world. We have to understand how participation online affects our off-line worldviews, and how not participating at all can be a negative social signal. We have to wrap our heads around how our digital spaces have been designed and what data is collected and why to understand the ethical implications of the tools we use. And we have to realize that the structure of the internet will continue to affect the structure of our businesses and that we have a stake in making our businesses better environments to operate in. For decades, digitally savvy leaders have been excited about the internet's positive potential to affect their businesses. But leaders who hope to transform their organizations won't get far without also acknowledging the internet's dark side.

The Reality-Distorting Effects of the Internet

In the spring before the 2016 presidential election, as I was preparing to transition the Organizing for Action (OFA) digital assets and exit the political arena for the private sector (and a much calmer pace of life), the FBI called our office to ask to come by and meet with us. We were honestly baffled by what they wanted to talk about, but my tech director and I agreed to take the meeting. A few days later, two agents came by our office and very politely asked us about our security protocols. They said they had intel that a hostile foreign agent was targeting our operation but couldn't say more. We gave them a rundown of our security measures, both from a technical and from a policy standpoint. They seemed satisfied and left. This encounter repeated several more times that year as the FBI checked in with us to make sure we were taking all measures to protect the president's online presence from interference. A few months later, WikiLeaks dumped emails from the Democratic National Committee that were stolen by Russian hackers in what turned out to be a successful attempt to manipulate news cycles against Hillary Clinton's presidential campaign.

Looking back, that moment in time defined for me the myriad of real risks we had ahead of us as an American society, where the security of our technology, the critical thinking of our media, and the socialization of our news cycles were all beginning to combine in ways that would cause real damage to democracy. The technology industry had up until that point had an almost mythological place in our society, with every other politician and industry leader scrambling to show how innovative they were by getting close to Silicon Valley entrepreneurs. President Obama himself did this: he developed meaningful relationships with Bill Gates, Mark Zuckerberg, Steve Jobs, and others while in office. Chris Hughes, one of the early founders of Facebook, left the then growing tech giant to join his 2008 campaign. Obama was routinely seen as tech friendly, both in policy and in practice.

SXSL, which would happen only weeks after my final meeting with the FBI, was maybe the president's final push to bring some startup culture to solving our biggest problems. Obama believed that technology could be an engine to accelerate progress, and that the tech-savvy, often progressive and idealistic, could be deployed in government and in the private sector toward meaningful ends. That thesis has been severely tested as scandal after scandal has dampened the glow of the tech sector and reduced the trust that Americans have in the industry.

In a Pew Research study conducted in the summer before the 2020 election, 73 percent of American adults said they were not too confident or not at all confident in the ability of technology companies like Facebook, Twitter, and Google to prevent the misuse of their platforms to influence the 2020 presidential election. A few weeks later, Pew would report that more than eight out of ten US adults go online at least daily, with 31 percent online "almost constantly."

As the final tally came in after the 2016 election, it became clear that Donald Trump would lose the popular vote by a historic margin. But many people who googled for the final results the week after the election were met with a piece of blatant misinformation as the top search result: a WordPress blog called *70News* screaming in all caps that Trump won both the electoral college and the popular vote majority. In 2017, users of Google Home, the company's voice assistant, could ask it if Obama was planning a coup and be met with a conspiracy theory that the former president was working with the communist Chinese government to overthrow the Trump administration. Google prides itself on providing the most useful information, wanting to be the "single source of truth" for the internet, but without some discernment on the part of the searcher, that "truth" can be far from true.

Perhaps the most egregious case of delinquency of duty to protect its users from misinformation belongs to Facebook. As early as 2014, Facebook leadership was bragging about its ability to manipulate the emotions of its users, participating in an emotional contagion study that showed how tiny tweaks to its News Feed algorithm could cause users to transfer both positive and negative feelings to each other. But in the run-up to the 2016 election, Facebook was walking back the claim it had any influence on the outcome. As I was having meetings with the FBI that year, in addition to their email drops, Russian hackers were dropping massive disinformation campaigns onto the Facebook platform, planting seeds of distrust in Hillary Clinton that would be amplified and re-amplified by Facebook users in the US. After the election, when the scope of the problem and how it had affected the election's outcome became clear, Facebook and other social media platforms made tweaks to protect people from paid disinformation campaigns by foreign entities. But Facebook barely changed anything about how its organic content spreads user to user. As I write this, the QAnon conspiracy is finding oxygen in the right-wing Facebook ecosystem, even as Mark Zuckerberg continues to deny Facebook's complicity in spreading falsehoods.

There now exists a real disconnect between the techno-utopian optimism of Silicon Valley entrepreneurs and the effects of technology on everyday life. Motivated by a dangerous combination of economic avarice and a progress-at-all-costs ideology, the tech industry has been both a democratizing force around the world and an enabler of antidemocratic behavior. Connecting the world has come with a lot of tangible good, including more access to information and education, more power for vulnerable communities, and better quality of life for millions around the world. But connection for connection's sake, even if leaders like Mark Zuckerberg genuinely believed it to be true, was never the self-evident good that it was sold to be. It turned out to be a pseudo-ethical means to the massive monetization of our attention. Companies like Facebook and Google are the original source of our Peter Parker syndrome because they have a stake in monetizing our outrage. They give us fewer shared facts in the name of "personalizing" our experience, and they provide us with the false impression that the personalization of our experience means the consequences of our actions online are also only personal.

I should note that this internet-driven reality distortion affects more than just our politics. I've personally consulted with Fortune 500 brand managers and CMOs in crisis mode over stories gaining traction on the internet about their companies that had no basis in facts. Social media crisis management has become a critical competency for any consumer-facing brand because of the propensity, the joyful proclivity, of internet hordes to "cancel" a brand because of a misstep whether that story reveals a deeper problem with the company or not.

I believe the accountability the internet provides for companies has on the whole been a good thing, as it is slowly forcing a marriage between words and deeds when it comes to corporate social responsibility. But it can go too far. When we read a story about a company, we are likely to look at the headline and we are likely to read and digest the points of views of our friends about the story. We are less likely to dig a little deeper and do the research ourselves to verify.

In 2017, the soap brand Dove released an advertisement on Facebook that caused a severe internet backlash. A Black woman was seen in the shower using the brand's products and then removed her shirt to reveal a White woman. Angry screenshots of the ad went viral, with many accusing the brand of invoking a racist stereotype that Black is dirty. The hashtag #BoycottDove was soon trending on Twitter, and the company quickly posted an apology and took down the ad. Many claimed that Black employees (if Dove had any) would have been able to call the ad problematic from the start, and the creative treatment was definitely a misstep on Dove's part.

But the screenshots weren't the entire story: in the full thirty-second TV commercial, seven women, each of different races and ages, removed their tops and changed into one another. Even the shorter Facebook version had the White woman turning into a Middle Eastern woman. If Dove's creative team, supporting a brand with a history of positive body imagery for woman, had reversed the order of the images, they never would have been called out. As it happened, the screenshots that circulated only showed the two Black and White women back to back—and for most of Dove's critics, that was enough.

The internet gives us access to the world's information, but we still don't know everything—and even when we do have information about a subject, it doesn't necessarily lead us to being more knowledgeable about that subject. We have a sense that we can find anything on the internet, we can know anything. And often we're desperate to know something. In extreme circumstances when we're desperate for answers, we're more likely to search atypical sources if mainstream outlets aren't able to provide what we're looking for.

The 2020 global pandemic, as an example, provided us with plenty of anxiety and few satisfying answers. The combination caused many conspiracy theories to become popular online, such as the claim that masks actually activate the virus or that Bill Gates created the coronavirus so he could use the vaccine to insert microchips in unknowing subjects. Conspiracies can feel more true than ambiguity in our search for comfort.

These are the reality-distorting effects of modern internet participation. Without the right types of education in digital media literacy so we can understand the sources of news delivered to us and the effects of filter bubbles—and respond with a healthy amount of critical thinking—we'll continue to struggle with healthy dialogue around our most pressing issues as a society. We amplify extreme points of view out of an emotional response to content algorithms delivered to us in order to get us to react, and the act of amplification reinforces our most extreme beliefs. The very act of sharing a point of view aligns our identity with that point of view, which reinforces the partisan nature of our public life in a massive cycle. And because we are most likely to amplify the worst parts of modern life, it's easy to feel like everything is terrible and nothing is ever going to change. Cynicism isn't just seen as cool on the internet; it's seen as somehow knowledgeable and savvy.

Participation as Existence

Alex, a friend of mine, was recently trying to take issues of social injustice seriously. He'd been struggling with how social media creates such performative expectations. The author Jia Tolentino, for example, has observed how on the internet, the expectation is to publish; if you don't post, you might as well not exist. This creates expectation—especially around significant, shared cultural events such as the George Floyd killing in the summer of 2020—that if you care, you'll speak out. Activists have critiqued this kind of social media–only activism as performative allyship and pushed back on campaigns like Blackout Tuesday, when scores of White people posted black squares on Instagram using the hashtag #BlackLives-Matter and silenced Black voices in the process.

Cognizant of that critique, and recognizing the effect the constant pressure to perform was having on his mental health, Alex decided to instead focus on taking tangible action. Instead of posting on social media, he started volunteering for local organizations working on injustice, and giving money to national Black Lives Matter movements. He didn't talk about any of this on his social accounts, preferring instead to do the work and not get specific social credit for it. He immediately began to feel like his work against racism had more integrity.

A few months into Alex's social media fast, a friend reached out with a long, heartfelt text message, saying she was disappointed in Alex for being so quiet. She wanted to see him speak out against injustice and felt his silence was complicity in the status quo. She said she'd have to take a step back and reexamine their friendship. Alex was shocked that the message came not in response to something he did, but something he didn't do.

The demand for internet participation is all-consuming in ways that we don't realize day-to-day. Participation—posting, consuming, sharing, liking—is an existential consideration. If we don't contribute to the great content machine, we risk irrelevance at best and outrage at worst when someone in our community moralizes our silence as a vote against progress. Once seen as a bastion of democratized information, the internet is now consumed with opinions because of how it has incentivized engagement for the sake of existence, and outrage is one of the highest forms of engagement.

Inflammatory content existed pre-internet, at least as far back as late-1800s yellow journalism and the circulation wars between Hearst and Pulitzer. But because of how the algorithms work on most of the internet, now the creation of inflammatory content actually provides us with social rewards: audience building, retweets and likes, and attaboys from friends. The journalist Charlie Warzel put it this way: "The absolute fastest way to grow an audience is to jump into a set of toxic, exhausted conversations and stake out a bold position usually at the expense of somebody else." This dynamic has been detrimental to democracy, turning our political identity conflicts up to eleven, but it rewards individuals willing to speak out boldly about something they're against. It's a tactic that has even become popular with brand managers: the food brand Steak-umm has grown in infamy by getting into Twitter beefs (apologies for the pun) about science with astrophysicist Neil deGrasse Tyson.

Combine the social rewards we get from dunking on others with the internet's ability to remember everything about our history, and we have created disincentives for ever changing positions. This is true of us personally: sharing publicly is the ultimate act of identity creation. But it's especially true for those in the public eye. We've always rewarded politicians and corporate leaders more for the steadfastness of their beliefs than the ability to change their minds (which gets painted as flip-flopping), but that has become especially true when there are past statements and video clips that anyone can dig up to ask, "This you?"

Despite the internet's increasing toxicity, I don't see our connected lives as necessarily negative. There are those, of course, who make the case that we should be able to delete our social media accounts, put away our phones, and get back to some version of humanity absent the surveillance capitalism that dominates most large tech companies. I sympathize with the instinct both to regulate large tech companies and to get back to the web's decentralized roots, and have advocated publicly for such, but assuming everyone has the choice to disconnect in today's world is naive at best. Careers are increasingly built with digital skills in mind, displayed on LinkedIn, maintained across a network of contacts made over years that would have naturally fizzled without its digital touchpoints. Social circles similarly are often maintained on social networks, sometimes made up of like-minded friends from around the world, often propped up with group texts or FaceTimes with family. To ask us to disconnect now is to ask us to give up career advancement and social capital. It's just not realistic.

Data & Surveillance

So far we've covered the human-to-computer interaction part of why the internet makes our modern lives so messy, but the backbone of the internet—the design of many modern digital products and their collection and usage of data—has been a point of ethical contention as well. For too long tech companies have operated with a "move fast and break things" mentality (the former mantra of Mark Zuckerberg and Facebook). Because of their desire for rapid growth, companies toyed with addictive user experiences and the collection and reapplication of first-person data in the name of *engagement*, a catch-all term to describe actions taken that prove the stickiness of a site.

Of course, the data they collect isn't used just to make these sites better for the users; it is used to make the advertising platforms smarter. Because of the ad-driven revenue models of the biggest sites on the internet, first-person data about the users of Facebook, Amazon, and Google has been compared by the mathematician Clive Humby and others to commodities like oil: a basic resource that once refined is incredibly valuable. Shoshana Zuboff, professor emerita at Harvard Business School, coined the term *surveillance capitalism* as a way to paint a picture of how Silicon

Valley and other corporations are mining users' data and shaping their behavior. This has led Chris Hughes and other advocates to propose a data dividend for users as a way to pay for the usage of their data. Others have advocated for at least more control over what is collected or for data ownership and portability.

Recently companies like Apple have leaned into a brand positioning around privacy, giving users new controls over the collection of their data across mobile websites and apps on the iPhone. Governments have started to step up as well: the General Data Protection Regulation (GDPR) implemented by the European Union in 2016 was a landmark line in the sand around data protection and privacy for any company wanting to operate in the EU. The GDPR isn't perfect—it mostly reined in third-party data collectors while requiring easily dismissible disclaimers on the collection of first-party data—but the EU has been far ahead of the US in terms of thinking creatively about the new data-driven economy and trying to get ahead of protections for consumers.

Despite the hype around data and the very real successes internet companies have had in harnessing it, many large companies are still behind in their data strategy. I've found that big data is hard for large corporations to wrap their heads around, especially when they are led by executives who aren't digitally native, who came up in the old world of business. But they're being increasingly pushed by the data-as-oil people to find and refine the pockets of information about their customers, their supply chains, and other areas of the business that could be incredibly valuable. The surveillance economy may be fired up, but realistically it's still just getting started for many large companies.

As the pressure builds on corporate executives to take advantage of surveillance capabilities, ethics experts are increasingly sounding the alarm over the collection and usage of data, arguing that many companies don't fully appreciate the nuances of its application. Organizations are collecting massive amounts of data points, passively from email to websites to social media and actively through surveys and other research tools. Often it is collected without consent, with no way for the user to correct or remove their data, and with no plan for how it will be safely stored or analyzed, much less destroyed appropriately. Organizations that move fast and break user trust will have to walk back their data strategy due to either government regulation or pressure from their customers. But those who figure out how to move quickly with due diligence will have less long-term risk to their infrastructure.

What's Eating the World

Data and surveillance is a major concern if we're ever going to build a new kind of conscious economy because it directly affects the profitability of some of our most influential companies. But I actually think the addictive nature of much of the internet, how it's been designed for maximum company value often at the expense of both individual users and society at large, may create more moral hazard for company leaders. Addictive user experience (UX), after all, is a microcosm of a larger company goal: keep them coming back. Entire libraries of design literature have been devoted to hooks, habit-forming triggers, nudges, and variable rewards that invest users in digital products. When it works like it's supposed to, UX creates trust between the company and its users, helping the latter navigate a company's products or services in a way that is mutually beneficial. Problems arise when UX becomes manipulative, creating an experience that nudges users in a direction that benefits the company at the user's expense.

Advocates for ethical UX have recently been trying to set some ground rules to make the entire industry more reputable, such as restrictions around notifications, transparency over recurring charges and the usage of data, and making it easier for users to opt out or cancel. These principles are a good start, but they don't address the harder tragedy-of-the-commons part of ethical design on the internet: how the design of one product may lead to unintended consequences outside of the company's control or understanding. Tech entrepreneur Anil Dash has spoken eloquently about the problems of scaling products without full ethical consideration: "Everybody in the Valley—they get their company funded, they make a startup, and they say, 'We desperately don't want to fail.' And I'm like—I'm not worried about the failures; I'm worried about the companies that succeed."

Facebook's News Feed may be the most prominent example of a product designed for maximum user engagement and satisfaction (and maximum data collection for Facebook's many advertisers) that has had massive societal repercussions. By learning about what a Facebook user wants to see, and then delivering more of that type of content instead of content that may challenge the user's perspective, Facebook created filter bubbles for internet information, reinforcing instead of challenging user beliefs. As Facebook became the number one source of news in the US, this had massive effects on the polarization of our political system that are still being felt today.

Leaders have to recognize a company's role in creating ethical standards for digital products: consumable content like text, graphics, video, and photography, but also websites, mobile applications, and software and the algorithms that power them. Understanding the ethics of data and user experience means implementing those standards systematically, operationalizing principles into products. It's not an easy task. Despite ethics being a cornerstone of business curriculum for years, in practice, most executives will always do what's best for growth and for the bottom line first. Companies looking to move with speed in an increasingly complex digital world will have to demonstrate a kind of creative thinking about the way they do business. We've done consulting work with clients who are interested in looking at not just a new business process, but a reformulation of the way they critique their own work internally as well, a way of constantly evaluating whether the tools they use to do their work are meeting the company's values.

In 2011, Marc Andreessen of the influential Silicon Valley venture capital firm Andreessen Horowitz wrote that "software is eating the world," making the prescient assertion that software companies were poised to take over large swaths of the economy. The operationalization of ethics isn't new, but the practice of applying it to the way digital products are being developed, especially by larger companies, is relatively nascent. If we're going to keep building a more inclusive economy, corporate leaders have to realize that digital products have special ethical considerations, including in the way they ask for and use data, and in the way they create addictive experiences for users. Software already ate the world. It's up to us to make sure what comes out the other end isn't shit.

Leading in a Connected World

It may be hard to read that I want you to focus on a more ethical version of digital transformation if your company is just getting started on its transformation to becoming a more tech-savvy organization, but that is part of the modern tension of leadership: when we know better, we have to do better. We've learned a lot about the right and wrong ways to create a digital economy over the past decade. The most innovative companies in the world right now are the ones that are constantly experimenting, constantly finding new areas of value, and ruthlessly shuttering business areas that won't serve them in the future. But few of even the most capable organizations are doing the work of digital transformation with an eye toward how a toxic internet environment is affecting their employees, or considering the ethical implications of the digital products they are taking to market. Many are still struggling with the basics of operating in a digital world, creating a new layer of complexity that most organizations are not prepared to address at all. That's a big part of the cultural lag we're feeling so strongly right now: even as the internet has increased moral hazard for the business environment companies operate in, many are still struggling with navigating a connected world in the first place. Digital natives are pushing society forward while institutional dinosaurs are just waking up.

Leaders have to recognize that employees have the same individualized connection to the world that consumers do, which means employees are also subject to the reality-distorting effects of the internet and also feel the pull to participate. That can mean participating in ways that make company leadership squeamish on a variety of fronts, including hyper-politicized conversations or conversations about the company itself. Employees are incredible ambassadors of their company, but the company has little control over what message those ambassadors are taking into the world. With some intentionality, those ambassadors can be an incredibly powerful resource for the company. (We'll talk more about that in chapters six and seven.) But first, leaders have to realize that their employees' connected lives don't end the moment they step foot on the company's campus. Leaders who try to keep their people from the world will find it an increasingly frustrating exercise.

In the spring of 2021, executives and cofounders of Basecamp Jason Fried and David Heinemeier Hansson, famous for their advocacy for a different kind of work culture, made a public declaration of policy changes at Basecamp written in a blog post. Among the announced changes was a declaration that they would no longer allow discussions of political and social issues at work. The internet exploded in outrage, with many people asking how such a policy could even be enforced (because what one person sees as political another may not), and others calling out that some marginalized people see their entire existence as inherently political. The company soon found itself in the middle of a media firestorm.

Some other company leaders, who were also struggling with how to manage employee fighting around social issues as an internal cultural problem, came out in defense of the new Basecamp policy. But the icing on the cake came when employees themselves started piling on publicly, accusing the leaders of taking unnecessary and arbitrary steps to end important conversations that were just getting off the ground. Soon other stories started leaking about a history of questionable behavior that had gone unchecked for years within the company walls, including a list of ethnic customer names employees sent around for fun. A week into the firestorm, Basecamp announced that a third of its employees were putting in their resignations.

If we accept the premise that our people are going to be connected, and are going to be participating in a potentially toxic internet environment, that means they'll be looking at how their company and its leaders participate for guidance. Leadership demonstrating a company's values externally does not just benefit its market presence; it also becomes a guidepost for employees looking for validation about their workplace and for how to be advocates on behalf of their work. That means that leaders can set the tone for engagement on potentially thorny political issues, demonstrating the rules of the road for the rest of the organization, instead of ignoring what is happening in the public square.

But if leaders truly want to make the internet environment less toxic, they'll direct their organization not just to help make their corner of it better, but to make the entire environment better as well. Individuals are the system components of the internet, but companies are the funding source for most of the major platforms through advertising revenue and other sponsorships. Right now we are witnessing a major tragedy of the commons, with every major company protecting its own corner of the internet without concern for how everyone else is doing. When leaders get serious about creating a better online environment for their customers, employees, and other stakeholders, they'll do more than advocate for it with their voices, they'll direct their companies to advocate for it with the power of their purse strings.

I don't write all of this to make you feel hopeless about our ability to make change in this reality-distorting world we live in. In fact, the opposite! I've never been more hopeful about the ability of a generation of new change leaders to transform society, change how we do business, and press forward our most important issues. Since I walked off the South Lawn in 2016 after SXSL, with all of those artists, techies, and entrepreneurs, I've become much more sober about the structural challenges presented by our digital ecosystem. But I think that's a good thing.

From a historical standpoint, the last few years have felt like the teenage years of the internet, when we realized our tech-leader parents don't actually have all the answers—and even in some cases may have given us the wrong ones. Now we're beginning to transition into our adult years and have the opportunity to create our own new identity. We have to start with acknowledging the challenges we face, and we especially have to be ready to be a part of the solutions.

The upside of recognizing that we don't share the same reality is that we can stop having needless arguments about what is factual, what is accurate, and what is true. Facts don't actually help us with persuasion as much as we believe they should. As I'll touch on later in this book, mind shifts in an internet world are possible but happen through micropersuasion, role modeling, and, most importantly, consistent and effective communication. For what it's worth, we should also have a healthy skepticism about our own perception and interpretation of facts.

Whitney Phillips and Ryan Milner, coauthors of *The Ambivalent Internet: Mischief, Oddity, and Antagonism Online*, have written eloquently about social media as a biomass pyramid, where the bottom strata of our small, everyday digital interactions, the ethically unmoored things we do without even thinking (posting snarky jokes about the news, retweeting misleading information even to condemn it, jumping into conversations without the full context, etc.) feed into the apex predators willfully harming or targeting other people online. "When applied to questions of online toxicity," they write, "biomass pyramids speak to the fact that there are far more everyday, relatively low-level cases of harmful behavior than there are apex predator cases." Without our amplification, predatory behavior loses energy.

We won't get answers by making technology more human or human centered, as some have claimed. The othering of humanity as outside of technology itself is actually another engineering-focused approach to what are essentially engineering-created problems, and puts the power to decide what is human and what is not into the hands of a few experts, continuing the Silicon Valley tradition of the consolidation of power. Tech has never been without the influence of the best and worst parts of humanity. Take, for example, the documented racial bias of most facial recognition algorithms. Humanity is also not a concept divorced from technology. We are shaped by the tools we use, and we use them to shape our world. As the philosopher Donna Haraway put it, we have always been cyborgs, hybrids of human and machine. This is what most developers miss about algorithms: they have persuasive influence on shaping our identity, even as flawed human thought seeps into the supposedly indifferent data that powers them. If we recognize that being technological is an essential part of being human, we realize the stake we have in shaping the technology industry.

It's time for our Spider-Man moment: we all have to take personal responsibility for what kind of world we want to see and recognize the power we have to make it either better or worse. But we also have to recognize that accepting responsibility for that power, accepting that it's up to us to make the kind of change we want to see, doesn't mean we'll ever see the end point or even know what the right end point is. This is the hard contradiction of modern life, in which the urgency of the moment and the constant swirl of digitally driven transformations combined can make us feel paralyzed. Our need for a point B, for some kind of port in the swirl, can keep us from taking the next step that's right in front of us. Making change in a digital world is possible, often elusive, and always harder than we realize it will be.

3

It's Hard to Grow in Public

I used to have a strange relationship with the Holy City—no, not that one, the one in Oklahoma.

In the foothills tucked away in a wildlife refuge near my hometown is a small compound called the Holy City, meant to replicate how Jerusalem looked in the time of Christ. The place is quintessential Oklahoma: surrounded by short grass, red dirt, longhorn, buffalo, and working-class grit. A few shabby clay buildings worn down by time and the wind off the plains are flanked by three life-size crosses at the base of the hills, looming large over the valley where desperate worshippers gather every year for the Passion pageant. The shabby grounds are all ambition with little delivery, but the nighttime viewing of the Passion provides just enough drama to pull it off.

I grew up in the Southern Baptist church, and that is the only way to describe it. When you grow up in the Bible Belt, you don't so much come to faith as you find yourself immersed in it from birth. Sure, there were conversion experiences—many in fact. Since the church put a singular emphasis on the number of souls saved, my friends and I came to Jesus many times, just to be safe. Growing up in that culture, religion was like fire insurance: something everyone had because everyone else said they should have it. And the annual Passion pageant, with its communal drives to mass conversion, was illustrative of that culture.

Questioning the teachings of the church at a young age was my form of rebellion, and it was a weak one, to be honest. Whereas other teenagers sought to distance themselves entirely from our soaked-in-religion culture, I was more interested in exploring it for its merits. I had faith. I genuinely believed what I read about this Jesus guy and what he taught. But I quickly developed skepticism about how those teachings were interpreted by my local church leaders, especially around social issues. Jesus didn't want us to have piercings or tattoos, apparently. Jesus cared a lot more about whether or not I was cursing when I spoke than about the poor. Don't even mention "the gays" around him. And he didn't want me talking to my nonbelieving friends, unless it was to evangelize. Be "above reproach," our leaders would say.

As I entered my teenage years, I became more disillusioned with their version of faith, and I attempted to push back. But our leaders, and even my church friends, would chide me for resisting their teachings, for testing the boundaries of my faith. I found it was hard to ask tough questions in an environment that was so monolithic in its approach to religious culture.

Revisiting the Holy City a few years out of college made me come to see it in a different light. My disillusion with the church hadn't stopped my viewing of the Holy City with nostalgic eyes. Maybe it was that the city wasn't owned by any one denomination or religious body but by the community. It was divorced from the institution of the church itself, instead becoming a place worshippers could find their own version of salvation. In one of the clay buildings, desperate people had filled the inside with their own inscriptions: calls for mercy, prayers for family members and friends, pleas for salvation. The earnestness of their asks to God always stood out to me, and as I returned to that graffitied building later in life, I realized that that was exactly what I was seeking: earnest exploration. A religion where I could be free to question, free to be a seeker, sometimes outside of the boundaries defined so acutely by my pastors.

The writer Frances S. Lee has written about the parallels they see between religious dogmatism and certain strands of social justice activism, including how both practice preaching and punishment. As someone who grew up in evangelical Christian circles and then spent time in political advocacy, I've seen both versions of this kind of ideological shaming. Political affiliation may be the closest secular equivalent to religion we have in the US. Professed belief in a set of doctrines is required for a run for office, especially at the national level. Rigid purity tests by both parties often leave no room for doubts or differing opinions. We create literal enemies out of those different from us, often equating their beliefs with evil. Growing up in a deep red state, I saw firsthand this us-versus-them dynamic, as insults were hurled at "liberal snowflakes" and "baby killers," and then witnessed the script flip when I moved to Chicago and worked in democratic politics against "heartless, warmongering idiots."

Whether or not they realize they're doing it, both churches and political parties often express cultural nuances that can be othering to the uninitiated. Cultural boundaries actually have little to do with right and wrong, as much as we want to believe that they do. Cultures form around doctrines as a kind of shorthand for beliefs so that we can quickly and appropriately categorize the people we meet. But the stronger the cultures become, the less room there is for nuance. When we're embedded in a culture driven by ideology, changing our minds can be a radical act.

In the previous chapter, we covered how the internet is structured in a way that isn't always helpful, constructive, or even ethical. But if we want to create more-just organizations, if we have any hope of making any kind of change, we have to wrap our heads around how much the internet has created a massive reinforcement structure for cultural boundaries, which makes it hard for anyone to process new information and grow into new beliefs. It's easy to convince ourselves that this only affects occasionally dogmatic institutions like religion and politics, but cultural conversations bleed into our work and our workplaces more than we want to admit. They affect employees and influence their interest in any kind of change initiative that may include cultural considerations. Mitigating the internet's negative effects on how your employees and customers perceive your organization and its place in society will set up any transformation effort for a better chance of success.

The Social Panopticon

In the eighteenth century, the philosopher Jeremy Bentham proposed a system of imprisonment called a panopticon. The concept was simple: people imprisoned would be positioned in a circular formation around a central station where guards could monitor them. The guards, however, would be concealed so that no one knew at any moment whether or not they were watching. This constant threat of observation, Bentham noted, would create better behavior, the basic idea being that the expectation of constant monitoring would create moral behavior through social discipline.

Philosophers like Michel Foucault would later critique Bentham's panopticon as a sort of power on autopilot, a tool of the elite to oppress not just through physical imprisonment, but through mental imprisonment as well. Foucault also extrapolated the concept of a panopticon to other areas of society, showing how in many social communities—our neighborhoods, our workplaces, our houses of worship—those in power use periodic monitoring to create social boundaries around normative expectations, creating a disciplinary society of surveillance. Who hasn't behaved just a little better when they're worried about their boss watching?

But what happens when it's not those in power monitoring us, it's us monitoring each other? Foucault talked about how normative expectations seep into our social communities in a way that causes us to monitor each other, but I don't think he ever could have conceived the scale at which that is possible in our modern digital age, nor the tools we would use to do it. Much of our social lives play out now in digital media, especially on Facebook in the US, which means that our social disciplining happens in imperfect forums where it's easy for us to misunderstand each other or read intentions into each other's actions that aren't there.

Social media increasingly reflects our IRL (in real life) friend graph (and then some) but the problem is that it's only a shadow of reality. The digital ethnographer Dr. Michael Wesch coined the phrase *context collapse* for the phenomenon that happens when we view content out of the original context in which it was intended—which, given the expansiveness of the internet, happens a million times a day. Typically communication between humans is an imperfect mess of interpreting body language, tone of voice, words, social context, and time, but on the internet we only have one of those things. The rest we are reading through foggy lenses, bringing a healthy dose of our own assumptions. Many times throughout the day we are reading and viewing intentions out of time and space, hearing our own voices in our heads do a poor impression of other people.

Social media has been called the highlight reel of someone's life, and I think that's a decent description. What we choose to publish often reflects what we want others to believe about how our lives are going. Yes, there are moments of real vulnerability that many of us also share, but even those are selectively chosen—out of necessity! Social media can never be fully reflective of our emotional ups and downs. We can't spend all day publishing about our lives when we have to go about living them. But this highlight-reel dynamic is creating a sort of moral hazard for those of us who want to speak out on any social or political issues. As we've already covered, our digital megaphones are some of the most consequential tools ever given to humanity, and we have to consider their applications as an ethical question. We also have to consider abstaining from their use as a question of balance between mental health and social responsibility. We all need a digital detox from time to time, but the decision to abstain from speaking out—to put down our megaphones—or even about what to post is an ethical one that we shouldn't take lightly. Our world's problems have always been interconnected, but now its problem solvers are as well.

There are also social considerations for abstaining, as my friend Alex discovered when he prioritized off-line over online activism. What conservatives have derided as virtue signaling is actually a helpful signal for most of us. We like to know when our friends share the same values as we do (and conservatives crying virtue signaling are sending signals themselves about their conservative credentials). Public displays of values convey reputability and reinforce friendships, relieving us of the need to "discipline" each other. They also give those of us displaying them a nice ego boost, whether or not we're conscious of it, because we get to feel like we're good people when we speak out about injustice. So from a social capital standpoint, public displays of values are a win-win—assuming you share the same values as your social network.

What Alex discovered is that we've reached a tipping point where because of post-to-exist expectations, communicating values and actually living values are two separate things that increasingly are collapsing in on one another. Whether or not we realize it, we often put expectations on each other about how we live our digital lives, or even the absence of living our digital lives. This can play out in innocuous ways ("Kenneth hasn't posted in months . . . I wonder if he's OK.") or ways that are more toxic ("Beth didn't post a black square! I can't believe she doesn't care about Black lives."). This may be the most panopticonic thing we do to each other, assuming the absence of moral statements is the absence of moral living itself, even though we never know the full reasoning behind the absence, or the capacity at which that person is operating in their personal life. We may be carrying personal tragedies, big or small, that make living in public difficult.

Discipline & Dogmatism

Public disciplining on social media is often derided as cancel culture, especially by those in power who are increasingly anxious about being held accountable by the public. The calling out of public figures in the past few years, and the subsequent piling on of the rest of the internet, has led to everything from uncomfortable conversations to losing work to jail time for those accused of bad behavior by the two most famous and most successful public accountability movements: #MeToo and Black Lives Matter.

But let's focus on peer-to-peer communication, where the practice of calling out has carried over into spaces where questions of power and platform are less applicable. Helping each other understand shifting norms and expectations, especially as relates to what we believe to be good and right from an ethical standpoint, is actually a useful social tool—and a big reason why so many intersectional issues have been brought to light in the past few years. As we've been flooded with the world's information, marginalized groups have been able to have their voices heard not only through their own accounts, but also through the amplification of the rest of us. To paraphrase Maya Angelou, now that we know better, we're able to do better, and we're able to ask each other to do better. But often the request to do better comes as more of a derisive command than an invitation, with a nice helping of shame on the side.

Loretta J. Ross, visiting professor at Smith College, has publicly called out call-out culture as toxic. As a Black feminist activist, Ross has lived at the forefront of social justice movements for four decades, including teaching anti-racism to women whose families were members of the Ku Klux Klan as part of the Center for Democratic Renewal, an organization founded by civil rights leader C. T. Vivian, and touring with Floyd Cochran, once the national spokesman for the Aryan Nations. She doesn't believe in public shaming. As part of her course White Supremacy in the Age of Trump, she teaches a module on calling in instead of calling out, encouraging her students to see mistakes as learning opportunities. She has related proving one's commitment to social justice to a varsity sport, and complained that the response to a transgression is often disproportionate to the original act.

"I think we actually sabotage our own happiness with this unrestrained anger," she said in a 2020 interview with the *New York Times*. Instead, she believes the practice of calling in should consist of correcting the person who has done something we believe to be wrong privately and with respect and then inviting them to behave better and get a deeper understanding of the issue. Importantly, calling in doesn't mean ignoring the behavior or pretending like harm wasn't caused, but it does mean adding compassion and context to the idea of inviting each other to do better. Vivian told her when she started her job at the Center for Democratic Renewal, "When you ask people to give up hate, you have to be there for them when they do."

The internet has created misaligned incentives for inviting people into deeper understanding. Not only are hard conversations hard to have online due to context collapse, but the rush of getting attention for calling someone out is sometimes irresistible—and often is, as Charlie Warzel noted, the best way to build an audience. Social media algorithms reward emotion and outrage, but they aren't sophisticated enough to distinguish between public shaming for big transgressions, and public shaming for small infractions. Plus, as a species we have little practice in the art of navigating public discipline given how new having this much global reach, this much power to influence each other, is in the context of history.

We have to recognize that when we invite people into social consciousness, we're not only inviting them into deeper personal understanding, but we're also asking them to step outside the bounds of their social context. We're often inviting them into a completely new culture, with new language, new rules and mores, new signals, and new expectations. Imagine you had no concept of the Christian church, no knowledge of the origin story of Jesus, and then were invited by a friend to join them in a service. You walk into the building and see violent symbolism everywhere: there is imagery of a man nailed, bleeding, in what looks like a *T*, positioned where everyone can sing to him. People keep talking about the blood of the lamb. To the culturally uninitiated, Christianity might seem unappealing, confusing, or even offensive. People new to the signals and expectations of being culturally conscious of marginalized groups experience a similar sort of culture shock and are often met with a similar ideological zeal.

The Christian missiologist and sociologist Paul Hiebert recognized this potential for culture shock and criticized many American churches for the way they unintentionally signaled exclusion to newcomers. Having studied mathematics as an undergraduate, Hiebert used set theory to explain his thinking: if we think of church communities as bounded sets of ones (the Christians) or zeros (the non-Christians), we are more likely to exclude those whom we don't consider our people based on expectations of which they may or may not even be aware. Does dressing a certain way, excluding certain words from your vocabulary, or practicing certain biblical disciplines make one more Christian than someone else? Jesus, according to Hiebert, didn't work that way. He wanted all to come to him regardless of cultural practice, regardless of whether or not they knew the "right" words to say or things to do.

Hiebert proposed a centered-set theory of a Christian mission instead of a bounded set of cultural expectations based on largely American ideas.

With Jesus in the middle as the ultimate end goal, the mission to which all signals point, all other religious practice could be understood in relationship to that mission. Some may be closer to the center, and some may be far away; some may be traveling toward it, and some pointed in the other direction. Hiebert thought churches should meet people where they are and go with them on the journey.

I've seen firsthand how social groups can shame those whom they see as less than pure. But if we apply Hiebert's thinking about how we go about the work of gently correcting each other, placing at the center the mission to do better and allowing for the other person to be on a journey toward that mission, we make allowances for people to come from where they're at, even while we call them in.

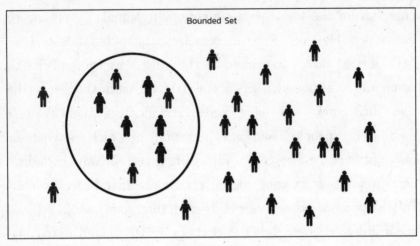

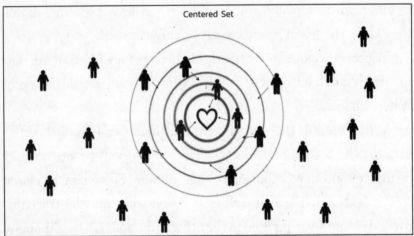

We don't have to believe their current position is tenable—in fact, we often know it isn't because we were once there, in their shoes, acting and believing ignorantly until we learned better and were able to move forward. I believe Hiebert's thinking can be applied in any situation in which we have a mission, so we can view people's commitments to that mission on a trajectory, rather than as a series of culturally bounded criteria.

Perils of Leadership

People in leadership—whether that be by title or by cultural influence—are especially susceptible to being called out because of the power and privilege of their positions. If you have a platform, if you have an audience of any size that listens to your opinions, expectations have changed for how you use that influence.

There are those who still get angry when CEOs, celebrities, sports stars, and other influencers don't "stay in their lane" when it comes to social and political issues, but those so-called lanes have always been social constructs. What we consider political especially has a different meaning for a White man than it does for a Black woman or a gender nonconforming person or an immigrant.

Increasingly, most of the public expects leaders to engage in public issues, especially those that are closely related to their work or their platform. (If you have a team of employees of any size, those issues are closer to home than you think.) But many feel that engagement in public issues is a minefield. How easy is it to say the wrong thing and have a social media mob ready to attack? As a business leader I understand that instinct, but often not engaging creates its own costs and its own moral hazard. Silence is in itself a political and ethical decision, one that often comes with risk.

The fear of being canceled is an understandable one because of the public's lack of sophistication in weighing the seriousness of transgressions—as we've already covered. We're new to this whole social-discipline-online thing and the internet's long-term memory. Once someone is canceled, stories can follow them for years, with internet trolls resurfacing stories every time that person pokes their head up. But I still refuse to buy into the idea of cancel culture being a net negative for society. People with any level of power and influence should be held accountable by the public, even if how the public holds them accountable is still unsophisticated.

The light the internet has shined on the dark places in society over the past decade has led to the toppling of some of the worst offenders who'd been operating with impunity for decades. If leaders and celebrities truly have nothing to hide, if they are operating with moral consideration as best they know how, they shouldn't fear the public's wrath. But they do need to know how to navigate it.

Occasionally, even those with the best intentions get it wrong. It's easy to step into a sensitive cultural issue out of ignorance or, in the case of those in leadership, to have someone you manage do it with you caught holding the receipt. We all have to be prepared to find out what we don't yet know. The world is too complex to expect perfection of ourselves or of others. We have to operate with moral imagination and expect that someday we're going to get it wrong. But getting it wrong and getting canceled don't have to go hand in hand if the transgression doesn't warrant it.

The first defense is a good offense; in other words, try not to fuck up and cause your own crisis. This means operating with moral integrity as much as possible, understanding that behavior by anyone in leadership needs to be beyond even the perception of impropriety. It also means maintaining tight control over your external communications.

When I worked on the Obama team, I had a mentor tell me the minute I joined that I had to start caring about everything. I was now working at the highest stakes of my career, and the smallest thing, even a typo, could potentially embarrass the president and cause a day or more of bad news cycles. Over the four years I worked for the president, I edited thousands of pieces of content, constantly scrutinizing them with my research and policy directors to determine whether or not a particular phrasing could be misinterpreted—and we were publishing hundreds of pieces of content a day across several platforms. We were operating at warp speed, managing one of the world's largest digital programs for the most powerful man in the world, and we were able to (mostly) do it without making any public mistakes.

If we could do it, I'm confident you can, too, but it takes some preparation and intentionality. You may not be operating with the kind of stakes we were, but you certainly are operating on the same global stage with the same potential for embarrassment, and you need to recognize that.

If an issue does come up, it can happen in several ways. Traditionally, public embarrassment of a company leader happens based on a real-world event such as a supply chain mismanagement or a C-suite sex scandal. In these cases, best practices for crisis management mostly still apply, with a few caveats. Whether or not you are directly involved in the scandal, you have to take responsibility and humble yourself before your customers, shareholders, employees, and the public at large, and overcorrect the mistake. But unlike traditional crisis management, responding in the internet age requires a speed and air of authenticity that is often difficult for the consortium of PR managers, lawyers, and C-suite executives that comprise a crisis war room to wrap their heads around.

In 2017, the internet exploded with video of a United Airlines customer being dragged off a plane after refusing to give up his seat on a full flight. Setting aside whether or not the policy of kicking off paying customers on a full flight was a smart one to begin with (see rule number one about a good offense), the company's response to the public's reaction to the incident turned confusion into full-blown outrage. Hours after the video had been circulating, the company tweeted a screenshot of a statement by then CEO Oscar Munoz that sided definitively with his employees and apologized for having to "reaccommodate" the passenger, apparently placing the blame on the customer.

The response reeked of boardroom groupthink, and, tactically, the attempt to use an old-world press release on a new internet medium invited mockery. Munoz himself tweeted a gentler statement a day later, but the damage had been done. When Munoz lost his planned promotion to chairman of the board a few weeks later, many jokes were made online about how he had been *reaccommodated* off the board. If the company had simply responded that they'd seen the video, were horrified by what had happened, and were looking into it, they would've bought themselves some time.

Increasingly, public scandals have nothing to do with real-life events at all but are born and bred on the internet alone, sometimes being picked up by mainstream media outlets that will then give them an air of credibility. As we've already covered, we are all managing the entirety of the world's information at once, and it's a lot to handle. If it feels like the internet is always mad about something, it's because we don't have many ways to manage the influx of things to be mad about. But for internet-driven scandals, a more cautious response by leaders is warranted.

Sometimes internet anger is like a firecracker, burning brightly for a short period of time before fizzling out. In those instances, and especially if the accusations are baseless, the vector of the conversation matters. If conversation is dying down, an interjection by the company will only give the outrage more oxygen—and the response by itself will be seen as legitimizing the initial complaint. I once had a food-service client respond to a baseless complaint in a Facebook comment not with a comment or correction on Facebook, but with a press release—which, of course, caught the attention of the national press and turned the complaint into a story.

If a conversation really is gaining momentum and there is a genuine critique behind it, such as the resurfacing of old comments that are being reinterpreted through a more modern understanding of an issue, the best thing to do is meet the moment head-on with humility. Acknowledge the issue and the critique, and commit to doing better in tangible ways. The best way to turn down the internet's heat is often similar to the best way to engage in conflict in person, but similarly to in-person arguments, so many people get into trouble either by being immediately defensive or by completely ignoring a legitimate complaint. The two golden parameters of internet engagement are authenticity and immediacy. The sooner you can answer with an as-human-as-possible response, the more people will give you the benefit of the doubt.

Of course, even the most humble of responses won't placate everyone on the internet, and there are those who will never feel comfortable giving people in leadership positions the benefit of the doubt. Some stories will last forever, both in people's minds and in internet archives. But you can't expect others to apply Ross's calling-in model of growth to you without first modeling it. You have to be willing to show yourself capable of growth, of hearing a critique and being moved by it to do better. If you can be a leader with the emotional intelligence to be able to apply humility to your own decisions, you'll be much more capable of tackling complex problems that require moral imagination. Sometimes the best response is to step out of the spotlight, to abdicate your leadership position in light of a scandal distracting from the ultimate mission. When necessary, admitting that past actions carry so much present baggage that it has damaged your leadership credibility and stepping aside is the ultimate act of growth.

Four Considerations

In many ways, it's easier to wrap our heads around how individuals get critiqued online than how companies or other institutional entities do. People have faces and names and are naturally empathetic based on our ability to relate to them on a human level. CEOs and other kinds of corporate leaders may represent their companies, but ultimately companies are faceless, complex entities, moving on multiple fronts like a multiheaded monster, rolling on like a machine with no one person able to fully turn it in any direction or explain all its moves. This kind of institutional complexity makes growing in public as a company even more difficult.

In the corporate world we talk about brand equity as the credibility a specific company or product has developed in the marketplace to be about something: quality, reliability, relatability, even social consciousness. How much brand equity a company has developed is a combination of internal and external factors. It's not marketing and communications alone. The repetition of specific messages over time is part of what helps develop an understanding of what the brand wants to be about, but increasingly the company's actions help determine how hollow or how solid those brand promises are. If a brand claims to be environmentally friendly, for example, but the company's corporate practices are actually damaging the environment, we as the public increasingly will notice the dissonance between what the company says and what it does. We are not likely to give companies not living their proclaimed values the benefit of the doubt.

Some brands have been able to develop lasting brand equity through a demonstrated commitment to social consciousness over time. Patagonia, for example, is well known as an outdoors brand that cares about the preservation of the outdoors and is willing to demonstrate that both in word and in deed, speaking out at key moments about policy decisions that affect the environment. It's willing to change how its products are sold as well. In recent years, the company has been pioneering a used clothing marketplace called Worn Wear as a way to reduce waste. Patagonia's history and brand positioning give it a lot of credibility to be able to engage in social issues that are directly related to its values. But how do you build brand credibility when your company has no history of commitment to an issue—and, in fact, may have actively committed to doing harm in the past? How can you turn a faceless corporate entity with a history of harm into something the public finds more sympathetic?

After the killing of George Floyd in the summer of 2020 and the racial justice protests that ensued, many corporate leaders spoke out about supporting the Black community and the need for American society to create a more equitable environment for all, including in the workplace. Even better, some announced public commitments to donations to organizations fighting for racial justice or teaching equity. But this time it wasn't enough: activists called on corporations to demonstrate their commitments not only through statements of public support and donations, but also through corporate practice, pointing out how monolithic many corporate boards and leadership teams are. Employees spoke out about unequal treatment in the workplace or, in some cases, called out specific managers who had caused harm. Just like the #MeToo movement had done a few years earlier, a reckoning came for companies that had created an environment that was toxic for their Black employees, even though some of those same companies had been posting in solidarity with the George Floyd protests.

We're reaching a critical moment where the daylight between corporate practice, corporate communications, and corporate positioning is becoming incredibly obvious. It is possible for large companies to become leaders in the new radically conscious economy despite any rocky history they may have with questionable corporate practice. But it's hard to grow in public. Corporate leaders have to approach the transition with humility, being ready to acknowledge past mistakes, and even more ready to admit current ones, on their way to a more just company. The nature of our internet-driven public discourse means that there will be plenty of people unwilling to forgive mistakes and plenty of people willing to call any turn toward more just corporate practice politically motivated. But it's not about politics; it's about principle.

What we consider political on any given day is a social construct that changes with the winds of our national narrative. Companies can't be afraid to do what's right for fear of it being politicized because any important issue is always going to come with that risk (and studies have shown that the risk of political boycotts is often more hot air than actual changes in consumer behavior). Any company willing to try to do better will find its customers and other stakeholders willing to go along on that journey with them.

But how do you actually begin to make change within the walls of a big, complex organization? In my work with 18 Coffees clients, I've found there are four major ethical considerations that a company should keep in mind as it charts a new course, and four major action steps.

Four Considerations	Four Action Steps
Employees	Create Ethical Boundaries
Operations & Supply Chain	Share Intentions Publicly
Customers	Constantly Communicate Values
Other Stakeholders & Communities	Plan for Failure

The first and arguably most underappreciated consideration is your employees, the people on the front lines of your business.

At the turn of the century, management thinker Peter Drucker counseled corporate leaders that the new generation of knowledge workers should be thought of more as volunteers, people who could take their knowledge somewhere else at any time, than as people with long-term loyalty to their organization. Therefore their contributions and opinions should be valued; companies should stop treating their employees as if the company was doing them a favor by employing them and start listening to their wants and needs. Even if you employ more than just white-collar knowledge workers, your frontline employees' opinions should be valued. They know your business better than anyone and are closest to your customer experience. They're also often treated the most poorly in wages and hours.

In the spring of 2021, when the American economy started opening back up as the coronavirus pandemic started to wane, many restaurant and hospitality industry managers complained about not being able to find workers to hire back. Many blamed the government assistance that had been provided to help people through the pandemic. But surveys of food-service workers by One Fair Wage and the Food Labor Research Center at the University of California, Berkeley, showed that three-quarters of workers cited low wages and tips as the reason for leaving their jobs, with others citing inhospitable environments due to the pandemic, such as safety concerns and harassment from customers.

It's no exaggeration to say you wouldn't have a business without your employees, so creating a good working relationship with them, opening lines of communication about their needs, and hearing what direction they see your company going in is the first step to running a more just organization. Employees can be your most passionate advocates or the first to call you out if your public statements don't match your practice.

The next consideration is about your behind-the-scenes operation and supply chain, the nitty-gritty of how you run your business, how your materials are sourced, and, importantly, what vendors you work with and what moral hazard comes with those relationships.

For decades, companies could get away with sourcing the most cost-effective materials from the cheapest labor all over the world using a see no evil, hear no evil approach to the ethical issues attached to that supply chain with maybe the occasional worry that an exposé or dogged journalist would reveal its dark underbelly. Now anyone with a smartphone and a Twitter account can be an investigative journalist. If the information is out there, there is always a risk of public scandal. And, admittedly, supply chain issues are some of the most difficult to solve, reaching deep into the global economy with ancillary political and economic issues across countries. Plus, no leadership team loves being in a position that requires it to raise prices while its competitors continue to exploit cheap goods and cheap labor. Evaluating your supply chain is about integrity, and it won't always come with an immediate market payoff. But the hardest decisions are hard for a reason, and doing the right thing without anyone knowing about it is one of the hardest.

The consideration that every business person understands, your raison d'être, is the customers: who they are, what they care about, and what geographies they occupy. Many businesses claim to obsess over their customers, but they obsess over a two-dimensional view of them. A consumer packaged goods company may love talking about soccer moms in the suburbs with purchasing power over family dinner as ideal customers, but it'd rather not acknowledge the ones that increasingly are concerned about the environmental waste related to its products. A sneaker company may love showcasing its relationship with Black athletes but not know how to respond when those athletes speak out about police violence in their communities.

Market segmentation at major corporations has for too long looked a lot like Hiebert's bounded set: a set of cultural expectations that help a company define the boundaries of a customer base without any nuance of the trajectory of that customer on cultural issues. Our new digital ecosystem means we now can have a more nuanced view of what people care about and try to meet them on that journey—or, even better, ask them to come on our own journey, toward our own mission. Standing for something more than just making money is an appealing place to be in a values-driven consumer marketplace.

Again, it's important to acknowledge that political considerations are going to matter here, and they're going to vary by geography. In the US our political conversation is so often nationalized, even when dealing with local issues, that a company listening to its local consumers runs the risk of drawing national attention from one side or the other.

In March 2021, when the Georgia legislature put in place new restrictive voting measures that disproportionately affected Black communities, residents of Georgia called on businesses based there, like Delta and Coca-Cola, to speak out. Many resisted until a consortium of Black executives put out an open letter condemning the act and rallied CEOs behind the scenes. When the CEOs of Delta and Coca-Cola did speak out against the new measures, they drew national attention from Republicans who condemned their "woke corporate activism."

Engaging in a political issue is never going to be without risk. Beyond the US, political considerations are going to vary region by region, state by state, which makes another case for companies to operate with clear values. No company has the operational capacity to engage in the important political considerations for each geographical area, nor should it. When a company's leaders have made clear what its values are and where it's going to engage, they help create a road map for standing on principle when local political winds shift.

The last consideration goes beyond your own customers and employees to other stakeholders in the geographies you serve. How do your products and your supply chain affect the communities in which you operate? For too long companies have myopically focused on their own operations at the expense of the environment around them, and that has caused real social harm. Sometimes it's environmental and tangible, like the smog from a factory affecting the quality of life for local families. But often it's the result of unintended consequences, products that were designed with specific users in mind without taking into account ancillary effects on other people.

Facebook's News Feed may be one of the most successful products in history with some of the biggest unintended social consequences affecting people who don't use Facebook, like the bifurcation of political news bubbles. Many thought leaders in the design community, which for so long has focused on human-centered design, or user-centered design, have started to focus on both users and nonusers, attempting to design with moral imagination.

The concept of a triple bottom line—people, planet, and profit—is one accounting concept that companies have used to attempt to capture their responsibility to external stakeholders. More recently, major investors have begun looking at the ESG framework to measure the societal impact of an investment in a company. Savvy investors are beginning to see that companies with society in mind have a better long-term financial performance and are beginning to evaluate executive compensation accordingly.

Four Next Steps

Once a company has done the hard work of considering the moral hazards its business model may expose, there are four major steps it must take to begin talking about its new direction publicly. The first is to decide what its ethical boundaries are and how it will operationalize those boundaries throughout the organization.

We talk about concepts like conscious capitalism and doing well by doing good as if deciding to operate an ethical business is like flipping a light switch, as if running a large business in a complex environment doesn't come with cascading ethical effects. Once we decide to open the door to ethical concerns being part of our decision set, we have to be prepared to make deep changes to our operations, some of which are going to come with compromise, some of which aren't going to make some stakeholders happy. But we have to do the work; otherwise, any public commitments that leaders make will quickly ring hollow when internet denizens dig up the myriad ways the company isn't living its stated values.

The second step is to draw a line in the sand regarding corporate practice, publicly, with teeth behind it. The mistake many leaders and corporate communicators make is to assume news cycles dictate moments of clarity for corporate values, when in fact it's the opposite. Corporate statements of solidarity ring the most hollow when no one has heard the corporate leaders speak out about an issue until it becomes major news—if Black lives didn't matter until they seemingly mattered for most people, for example. Leaders who publicly make commitments outside of news cycles are declaring that something is so important to them that they are willing to make it a news cycle, willing to risk all the spotlight on their commitment instead of it washing away in the ebb and flow of the social tides. Patagonia didn't get a corporate reputation as an environmental activist because it picked a select moment when the environment was in the news. It got that reputation for making sure the environment stayed in the news.

Those with skin in the game early will always have more credibility than those who waited until it was socially convenient to take a stand. Don't get me wrong—if no commitment to an issue has been made and a #MeToo or George Floyd moment happens, it's always better to listen to the internet feedback and decide what principles your company wants to stand on before it's subject to a mob backlash. But if you're late to consciousness on an issue and sticking your neck out only when everyone else does, your public commitment had better be substantial. The third step is that you constantly have to communicate your values and priorities. It's not enough to draw a line in the sand once, to put specific words up on your website and expect that to communicate on your behalf for all time. A commitment requires both follow-through and public storytelling about that follow-through. As we'll cover in the next chapter, narratives are built through consistency, through finding micromoments of engagement that demonstrate values through repetition. Repetition creates credibility, and credibility creates public equity that leaders can draw on when living their values inevitably gets hard. And it will get hard.

As the fourth and last action step, companies need plans for what happens when they fail. The application of ethical principles in complex environments is going to get messy. Something is going to go wrong. The mob-like internet's unsophisticated feedback can roll over the unsuspecting like a tide, but as someone who's worked in internet environments for most of my career, I actually have a more nuanced view of public engagement than you would expect.

On the internet, the loudest, most outrageous voices tend to get the most engagement, but I believe most people are able to forgive companies that are willing to make an effort. As long as a company that has screwed up in a messy public way applies the rules of crisis management (admit the mistake with humility, overcorrect, and commit to doing better), the equity it has built with the public through consistency on an issue can override a misstep and drown out those who have no willingness to forgive. But consistency is key. Without an already demonstrated commitment to an issue through both words and actions, missteps and scandals create reputation holes that can dog a company's brand for years. It may be hard to grow in public, but the public respects those who are trying more than those who have chosen the ethically dubious position of the status quo.

4

Narrative Is a War of Attrition

Climate change is the most important issue that represents the disconnect between short-term urgency and long-term apathy. That is true today, and it was true in 2014 when I was working on a campaign to refocus the American public on the issue. In just a few years, President Obama would sign the Paris Agreement, committing the US along with the rest of the international community, to ambitious climate goals. But in 2014, our Congress was still full of climate change deniers, which had led to crippling inaction on the issue for decades. The scientific community had long ago come to a consensus about the issue, but political realities in the US meant that many politicians could skirt the issue, cater to lobbying by the fossil fuel industry, and not face consequences with their voters, who often cared more about the kitchen table issues right in front of them.

My social media team at Organizing for Action (BarackObama .com) had spent the last couple of years perfecting an approach to online engagement that prioritized setting a narrative early, distributing that messaging to our thousands of volunteers, and then working with them to repeat it often to make sure it became the narrative that entered the political bloodstream. Despite aggressive pushback from right-wing pundits and online trolls, we had successfully seeded online narratives around health care, equal pay, immigration, and other issues important to the president that became the dominant framing for those issues on social media.

In late 2014, we set our sights on showcasing just how many members of Congress still denied the science of climate change. We worked on three fronts: as my digital team focused on creating content, our policy and partnerships team worked to mobilize the environmental advocacy coalition, and our organizing team distributed messaging and instructions to our volunteers. Working with partners around specific issues—partners who didn't always see eye to eye on our approach—was an important part of mobilizing an entire coalition around messaging whenever we wanted to lead around an issue. And creating moments around specific dates focused the organic online conversation in a way that made the social media algorithms recognize those conversations as being important. The result was that we were able to get the phrase *climate change deniers* into the lexicon in Washington and create political space for President Obama in the run-up to the Paris Agreement.

Not only did we see spikes in conversation around climate change denial on the key dates around which we had mobilized, but we also saw climate change denial eventually overtake other environmental topics in our social listening data. We even saw journalists begin to use the phrase when talking about specific politicians in the mainstream media. Our success was determined not only by our ability to mobilize so many actors to change the way they talked about an issue, but also by how often the new message was repeated across the internet.

We may have pioneered that model, but over the next few years it would be co-opted by politicians, campaigns, pundits, and internet outlets on both sides, all of whom had a stake in setting the narrative around specific issues. With the growing influence of the internet on the mainstream media's focus, it would become a powerful tactic—and table stakes for any campaign or company looking to break through the distributed nature of today's media environment.

Reality and Online Reality

Fiona Godlee, the editor in chief of the *British Medical Journal*, was exasperated with the *New York Times*.

At the end of 2020, faced with a surge in a new variant of coronavirus infections and now armed with two newly developed vaccines, the UK issued new guidelines for vaccine distribution. They included a provision for mixing and matching vaccine regimens under extreme circumstances, such as a case when a high-risk person showed up without any documentation about what first dose they had received. The guidelines explicitly asked that "every effort should be made to determine which vaccine the individual received," but rather than leaving the person with no booster whatsoever, they suggested "it is reasonable to offer one dose of the locally available product to complete the schedule" because both vaccines are "based on the spike protein."

Giving two different vaccines hadn't been studied, though some pointed to evidence that giving two separate types of vaccines may work just as well, if not better. (When boosters began to be administered in the fall of 2021, any type of vaccine was recommended, not just a third dose of whatever vaccine was originally administered.) The thinking was that two different shots was better than no booster, especially for those "at immediate high risk or unlikely to attend again" as the guidelines stated. The CDC in the US had included the same recommendations for the same extraordinary circumstances in its guidelines.

When the new guidelines were released, the *New York Times* ran a story with the headline, "Britain Opts for Mix-and-Match Vaccinations, Confounding Experts," with quotes from several scientists and academics questioning the wisdom of mixing and matching. "There are no data on this idea whatsoever," one expert said. The article made the rounds of the social media outrage cycle, shared by livid UK politicians and scientists who used the story as more evidence of the incompetence of Prime Minister Boris Johnson in handling the crisis. Many were surprised that they were hearing it from the *Times* and not from the British press.

Godlee was livid and demanded the *Times* print a "highly visible correction," pointing out how the title, often shared with little context, had damaged public trust in the vaccine rollout. She told the BBC that the headline had been "seriously misleading." A correction wasn't issued, but there was a slight change in the title

("Britain Opens Door to Mix-and-Match Vaccinations, Worrying Experts"), and a quote was added from health authorities noting the rare case when a substitution would be warranted.

A horde of Twitter users piling onto a story that isn't exactly true isn't a novel internet experience by any stretch, nor is the sharing of a sensational headline without context. But the experience was indicative of our tendency to read what we want to read into a story—in this case, the incompetence of Boris Johnson and right-wing politicians in the UK—and the unconscious ways we bring our group instincts into our interpretation of the news. Most of us (journalists included) like to believe that we bring an objective view to how we see the world, but, in fact, most of us approach our interpretation of events with a degree of what psychologists call naive realism: we believe we're viewing events objectively, and those who disagree with our views are either irrational or uninformed. The effects of naive realism, combined with confirmation bias and strong loyalty to our own cultural social groups, have always been pronounced in our interpretations of reality. Combine that with algorithms of outrage and (let's be honest) our tendency to not click through and actually read the articles we're sharing, and we get a recipe for an interpretation of reality that is machine-made for just our worldview.

The field of communications has always been a blood sport, with various parties fighting to control the narrative as the most honest media gatekeepers struggle to interpret events in the most objective way possible. But our new socio-digital reality means that the gatekeepers have been dispersed just as our level of information has exploded. Making change in today's world requires even more attention to the communications and media ecosystem, even more investment in consistent messaging than ever before, because our realities have been split into a thousand pieces personalized to just our taste.

In a paper released in July 2021 called "Stewardship of Global Collective Behavior," a group of researchers argued that we should start treating social media as a crisis discipline similar to climate change or public health. Any company leader wishing to create, maintain, or evolve a brand reputation has to understand the resources and dedication it will take in the kind of internet environment we have. The war for reality often requires us to operate in ethical gray areas and make hard decisions at a dizzying speed.

Micropersuasion

Communications professionals used to launch campaigns in a pretty linear fashion: planning, launching, making iterations if necessary, and evaluating what worked and what didn't. Most companies just can't afford that kind of space and time for engaging with the public anymore. Social media has dramatically shortened the consideration and planning period to the point where most communications planning happens in a matter of hours, if not minutes. Maybe on some of its most important non-news-cycle-dependent initiatives, a company can create a moment from nothing, but it has to spend that kind of capital wisely, and it takes a lot more repetition to break through the thousands of messages people get every day in a dispersed media ecosystem.

It's easy to become incredibly reactive in this kind of environment and to think the biggest opportunities are to ride the right kind of news cycle into legend. Indeed, some brands have been able to create moments out of pop culture convergence. One of the earliest and most famous examples of brands doing this was the "You can still dunk in the dark" response from the Oreo brand to the 2013 Super Bowl power outage. The success and notoriety that response raised for the Oreo team's ability to quickly think on its feet, produce content, get it approved, and respond while the moment was still relevant caused a flurry of copycats. It birthed a real-time marketing movement that saw brands weighing heavily into cultural moments—that is until a few years later, when the majority of cultural moments on social media became driven by political outrage.

Real-time marketing and its descendant tactics may have been a transparently desperate attempt by some companies for relevancy, but the basic idea of moving quickly, tightening the cycle between idea conception, approval, and deployment, was solid, and savvy companies have taken note.

Digital not only demands responsiveness, it also creates learning opportunities for those willing to listen. The timeline for campaign planning has been condensed, but the smartest communication strategists see that as an opportunity for testing and learning. Previously, campaigns were deployed like an ocean wave. Triggered by certain criteria, they would build momentum and strength until finally breaking the surface and crashing into the shore. Now we can deploy microcampaigns across different platforms like a thousand separate wave pools, testing different versions of messages through paid and organic media, gathering data about what stakeholders want to hear and what messages are most persuasive. By the time we're ready to execute a larger messaging campaign, we should already know what works because we have the data to prove it. The best metaphor I've found for this new way of seeing the world is how the crew of the *Nebuchadnezzar* views the Matrix in the movie of the same name. Through a series of individual lines of code, each telling an individual story, an entire world comes into view.

21st Century Campaign Planning

Linear planning cycle	⟶	Constant learning & iteration
Strict market definitions	⟶	Flexible market definitions
Operational rigidity	⟶	Operational flexibility
Unchanging value proposition	⟶	Evolving value proposition

Operationally this can be a hard concept to grasp for organizations used to operating like big, complex bureaucracies, and who aren't used to the risk exposure of social media. When deploying a thousand punches, one is bound not to land right. Especially in the hyperconscious media environment in which we find ourselves now, it's understandable that some executives would want to slow down the process and make smart decisions. But too often those decisions are made by committee, with decision makers in various places (some of whom may not even be in the building, like an agency), causing the company to miss critical opportunity windows for cultural moments or crisis management. Senior executives who have become wise to the importance of digital communications increasingly have their hand on the wheel but don't always have a savvy enough understanding of the demands of internet culture to know how to navigate. I've also seen companies that still do the opposite: hand their most important communication mediums off to junior-level employees (or even interns!) without much support from management, often under the guise of those employees being more digitally native anyway. Inevitably, a crisis will end up exposing how unprepared and unsupported those employees were, and those same leaders will expect a quick fix to the problem that could have been avoided.

An operational balance has to be struck between speed and good governance. What that right balance is for every organization is different, but it involves the same elements: clear communication and workflows, understanding of roles and responsibilities, and a predetermined strategy that everyone has bought into across the organization. Often this means a completely new operating model.

As my friend Michael Slaby, former chief technology officer of the Obama campaign, used to say, operating with digital savvy isn't complicated, it's just hard. It requires cross-functional collaboration and decision-making at speeds that tend to push traditional org charts to their breaking point, often causing tension between C-suite leaders and their team members. Attempting to operate in the new digital world with old-world infrastructure—whether that be technology or human—is a recipe for ineffectiveness at best, and public disaster at worst.

Ultimately, operational effectiveness matters because effective marketing is about repetition. While we're running microcampaigns, testing out different messages and investing in the ones that work, we're also testing the frequency at which people need to hear a message in order to be persuaded. We've known for a long time that people have to hear a message around seven times for it really to sink in—an old advertising adage—but what most traditional marketers could never have anticipated is the sheer number of messages the digital age throws at us every day. Repetition is happening so much in so many places that we're becoming oversaturated.

We also are not the main gatekeepers of the message for the most part. The algorithms are. By creating news feeds that are attempting to give users what they want to hear, or in Google's case what it thinks is the right answer, the platforms are ensuring only certain kinds of messages get repeated. Content on Facebook, for example, goes further if Facebook users engage with the message (like, share, comment)—but even when we don't engage, we still see the headlines that others in our network think are important. We are still touched by the message, still influenced by our social circles.

Tech companies like to believe their algorithms are value neutral, but they underestimate their persuasive influence. By guessing at what people want based on past behavior, they can unintentionally reinforce people's worst instincts instead of nudging them toward their best. One prime example of the negative effects of algorithmic persuasion came to light after the January 6, 2021, attack on the US Capitol Building. It was discovered that many of the rioters were organized via Facebook groups and that many had joined those groups based on the suggestion of Facebook's News Feed. Algorithms are not value neutral, and more recently there has been a push by data scientists and ethicists to regard the data inputs into algorithms as an ethical consideration.

Until our tech ecosystem becomes healthier, we have to figure out a way to work within it, to game the gatekeeping system in order to penetrate it with messages we believe people need to hear. Some have called for abstaining from digital platforms or boycotting companies to make a point about toxic online culture, but that only works to make a point in the short term. Long-term abstaining only cedes the messaging ground to others, allowing other often ill-intentioned voices to set the narrative around an issue. No one enjoys using the tools of war, but this is the battlefield we've been given, for now. I believe abstaining completely from online discourse maintains the status quo at best, and allows for persuasion in negative directions at worse.

What we're ultimately doing day-to-day through our micropersuasion campaigns is reality building. When we're met with so many competing interests but fed back the ones tech companies think are meant for us, each individual has their own version of world events. No one's Instagram feed, Google results, Twitter topics are the same. Everyone's Venn diagram of shared facts overlaps in subtle ways, but sometimes the unshared area can be dramatic, especially based on our political media diets. Reality itself has always been interpreted through personal experience and unconscious bias, but now we have an extra lens of personalized entertainment and information that distorts our perception and contributes to the problem of naive realism.

If you are truly to go about the work of changing perception on an issue, whether that be advocating for something you care about or even just creating positive associations with your company, you have to use the tools of the digital dystopia we find ourselves in, even as you try to make that environment slightly less dystopian. You have to fight for reality as you see it, or else the war is lost.

Storytelling in a Digital World

In October 2017, fast-food chain Kentucky Fried Chicken announced a new UK partnership with the global logistics and shipping firm DHL, promising to revolutionize the food-service supply chain with a focus on reliability. The partnership didn't start well. Within weeks of taking over delivery management from the previous logistics firm, DHL struggled to fulfill its obligations. By February of 2018, KFC restaurants across the UK were running out of chicken as well as other important ingredients.

More than nine hundred KFC locations were forced to close, and the others faced irate customers frustrated at what they saw was incompetent management, not a supply chain issue. The story caught the attention of the global press. Upset customers were more than happy to give interviews on top of tweeting their frustration. The hashtag #ChickenCrisis began trending.

To turn the disaster around, KFC set out to do two things without blaming its new partner, DHL: issue a massive apology to its customers and explain what was happening behind the scenes to fix the issue. The leadership team knew it had to do more than issue the normal bland corporate apology given the skepticism of the UK public. They decided on a simple approach: place two advertisements in the widely read newspapers the *Sun* and *Metro* that featured simple language apologizing for the missteps and directing readers to a microsite with further explanation. The ad featured a hero image of their iconic chicken bucket with the letters of their name rearranged into the word *FCK*.

The ad caught the attention and imagination of not only the UK public, but the global community as well. Over the next week, more than seven hundred media mentions and 219 million social media users discussed how the brand had used humor to diffuse an embarrassing situation. By some estimates, the ad received over 1 billion impressions. Over the next few months, customers gave the employees much more benefit of the doubt about the causes of the issues as operations eventually returned to normal and locations opened again with full menus. The incident did no lasting damage to KFC's reputation. In fact, data from YouGov's BrandIndex at the time showed the brand with an incredible resiliency among its customers.

Meghan Farren, KFC's CMO for the UK and Ireland, told the UK's *Campaign* magazine that they didn't set out to do something so huge or impressive. "If you want people to connect with other people," Farren said, "you are authentic and open and honest and humble. We just acted like that."

How do you tell a good story in pieces? The ultimate challenge of any communicator in the modern digital age is that every piece of content has to both be part of a larger narrative and live on its own without us assuming that anyone sees the bigger picture. We have to apply complexity thinking—the idea that systems have to be simultaneously considered as whole ecosystems and the sum of their parts—to something that has traditionally been a pretty linear discipline. Stories have a beginning, middle, and end; characters, exposition, and climax. If we're trying to set a narrative across the digital divide of space and time, when any piece of content can be read out of context of the whole story, we have to build some elements of story into its pieces.

I've already mentioned repetition as one of the most important tactics, especially if particular parts of the story are more important than others. But effective communication teams do this kind of story diffusion in a variety of ways, not just with words. Good visual design, with design elements (not just logos) like colors, icons, and imagery that repeat across different pieces of content, can trigger an unconscious recognition that different pieces of content are related. But the words themselves do matter as well.

As all good writers know, effective communication requires creating a specific voice, creating artificial boundaries for characters that make sense as part of their story. A company is no different. It has to know what it will say, what it won't say, and what is authentic to its brand. Often companies will create voice documents that outline those boundaries for use by multiple writers. Then for any specific campaign or initiative, marketing teams will often create copy decks that give messaging guidance that can be customized for different mediums. Each platform has its own culture, its constraints providing important strategic guidance and its audience having specific expectations about how one should engage. Customizing a story for that specific platform is always a good idea.

Again (and again), repetition matters. Part of the answer to the challenge of communicating across time in different pieces of content is that people have to read the same messages repeatedly in order to digest them. That was true in the predigital marketing world, and it's still true today, when thousands of messages are competing for our attention. Repetition also matters when we're trying to communicate across multiple platforms with different audiences. If someone receives an email, views a TikTok, and watches an ad all from the same company about the same issue, how the company ties those messages together into something coherent is key to making them stick.

There's a famous lecture by Kurt Vonnegut that has guided my thinking on content strategy and storytelling over my career. The author talks about the familiar narrative arcs of Western stories that give them their shape over time. Standing in front of his students, Vonnegut literally maps the fortunes over time of protagonists from famous stories on a timeline plot. In "boy meets girl," the arc swings into good fortune as the romance is kindled, only to turn back into ill fortune as some inevitable conflict occurs, until finally, at the climax of the story, the ill fortune is turned around and the couple live happily ever after. A similar arc occurs for a "man in hole" story, where a protagonist has to overcome an obstacle and ends in a better place after the experience. A more dramatic fate befalls Cinderella when the clock strikes midnight, which Vonnegut illustrates with a straight line falling into ill fortune all at once. Vonnegut's point is that some story arcs have been told repeatedly over time, and the repetition has made them comfortingly familiar to us. We expect a good story to go in a certain direction.

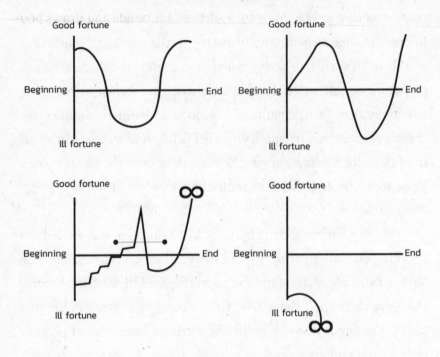

I believe good content strategy and narrative building around a change initiative has to be similar. If a company is trying to turn something around—whether that be its own behavior or a bigger social change for which the company is advocating—it has to be clear about who the protagonist in the story is, where the arc of the story is going, and what conflict is going to be overcome. Are we the audience part of helping the protagonist overcome their obstacle? Or, better yet, are we part of the protagonist group ourselves? As a story about change unfolds, having that kind of clarity can help shape the kind of story you tell over time. The FCK campaign had a clear "man in hole" arc: the protagonist, KFC, had found itself in ill fortune, and we as the audience got to be part of rooting for the protagonist to overcome it. Having clarity on the shape of the story can help create a content cadence that builds and draws people toward taking action.

Riding the Wave

Calls to control the narrative have been a part of public relations for decades. But controlling a message in our internet-driven culture, where stories spread like wildfire, often across multiple sites and often invisibly through word of mouth on messaging platforms, is functionally impossible. Companies often aren't the ones breaking news about themselves, and when they do, they don't have as much ability to work the refs—that is, build relationships with friendly journalists who can put a spin on a story favorable to the company. There are simply too many gatekeepers now. Some journalists, especially in certain industries, still have platforms that can demand the kind of internet attention and respect to make their versions of events the story. Often those journalists have built audiences not only through newsrooms but also individually through Twitter, newsletters, or podcasts. Those journalists are the least likely to be spun. They've earned their respect for a reason.

The PR firm MSL has created a model for how stories break in our internet-driven environment. Three separate but related types of news waves come after an event. The first type follows a more traditional model of breaking news: something happens in real life, the mainstream media covers it, microblogs like TikTok and Reddit react, and eventually interest dies down as think pieces and long-tail analyses start to put the event in context. The second is internet first: an event happens, and someone online calls it out or showcases it. Mainstream journalists then catch up to the story just as it's gaining traction with Twitter, and the analysis of traditional journalists may or may not take hold in the internet conversation before the narrative is set. The third version is the most unique to our moment in history and the hardest to manage from a reputation standpoint: stories that start online and stay online, never touching the mainstream. These are the rumors, the partisan myths, the anti-somethings based more in fear and loathing than they are in fact. They can start several ways, including intentionally or unintentionally misinterpreting legitimate news stories. Internet news articles such as the analysis of a partisan blog with a sensationalist headline being shared around as gospel can be their cornerstone. Or they can just be whispers and innuendos. Respectable journalists often will not touch these kinds of stories except to occasionally debunk ones that seem to be getting a lot of traction, which means they can linger in the consciousness of the internet for a long time.

One of the most active and most insidious of these kinds of narratives in recent memory is the QAnon conspiracy theory, the kind of internet frenzy that was custom-made to meet the political moment of the Trump presidency. Vast swaths of the conservative internet, looking for reasons to support their hero president, were attracted to QAnon not necessarily because it offered answers, but because it raised the right kinds of questions about their perceived enemies. Its assertions (that Donald Trump was secretly fighting a Democratic politician–driven child sex ring, among other things) were just the kind of confirmation of their hate the supporters were looking for. QAnon and similar rings of extreme right-wing online organizing were part of the reason the US Capitol was attacked on January 6, 2021, as online narratives spilled over into real-life violence.

For a few reasons, we as a society don't yet know how to tackle these kinds of insidious online narratives that capture the imagination of certain parts of society. One is that we're still not paying attention in the right places, or seeing how all the pieces fit together. Because much of the conversation happens on private forums, researchers, law enforcement officials, and others who may be interested in tracking the trajectory of the conversations only have so much exposure to them and have to rely on the cooperation of the platforms for insights, which itself raises privacy concerns. If ethnic violence is being coordinated on private Facebook-owned WhatsApp groups through encrypted messages, for example, as it has been recently in India, Israel, and other countries, Facebook may have only a degree of visibility into those group conversations even if it wanted to coordinate with law enforcement. This is the downside of a connected society: we've given the darkest human instincts the ability to organize online, which makes them more organized off-line.

Another reason these kinds of conspiracy theory–driven narratives are hard to fight against is that the usual tools of narrative only work to a certain degree. Third-party vetting of a story by a credentialed journalist or influencer (like a politician or business executive) often only confirms the story's validity within communities naturally skeptical of mainstream institutions. People willing to cry conspiracy see the conspiracy everywhere, especially in the response of those perceived as involved in it. Any negation of it tends to give it more oxygen, tends to confirm the very thing those bringing forth facts were trying to debunk. Psychologists call the reinforcement of core beliefs in the face of conflicting evidence the backfire effect, and on the internet it happens on a massive scale every day.

The scale itself is the issue—and the solution. Deconstructing false narratives is both a centralized mainstream media problem and an individual problem. It's something you and I have to own ourselves as part of a global system of information flow. We need credentialed journalists and experts to help guide those of us who see ourselves as critical thinkers to higher levels of truth, but many of those around us are never going to respect the credentials of those we listen to like they're going to respect our opinions. Our friend-ships, our shared histories have given us relational equity with the people around us, and when it matters, we can trade on that equity to help them see a different perspective. It doesn't mean we shout in their faces or make demands of them they're not capable of meeting at that moment (as we've covered in the previous chapter, that can be counterintuitive). But it does mean we make an effort to use our own voices, online and off-line, to intentionally provide a different perspective. The organized application of individual influence has to go hand in hand with the megaphones of the experts.

As a company leader, narrative building in this way is para-mount not only to pushing back on false stories, but also to provid-ing a buffer for the kind of public growth we've already discussed is critical to operating as an ethical organization. We have the tools now to activate our most passionate advocates to be fact-checkers on our behalf, to provide third-party credibility for our company's growth trajectory when we screw up, but they only work if we use them. This is where the diffusion of social media can play to a company's benefit: customers, employees, and other stakeholder advocates can act as a small army of actors on the narrative battlefield, pushing back against company detractors but also distributing positive news at appropriate moments. If narrative is a war of attrition, you have to be constantly putting out small-scale and large-scale content that creates the kind of narrative you need to win the war.

Andreessen Horowitz, the fabled venture capital firm famous for investments in Airbnb, Facebook, Skype, and others, recently deployed this kind of content mobilization across multiple platforms with multiple stakeholders on behalf of its portfolio companies—including Coinbase, a cryptocurrency trading platform that had come under scrutiny from tech journalists for its treatment of Black employees in late 2020. Rather than allow the narrative to be set for them, Andreessen encouraged Coinbase to strike back and tell its own story and deployed an army of techies and crypto influencers to back them. So much animosity developed between some tech journalists and some Silicon Valley leaders that Andreessen launched its own multimedia platform to take the story of its companies directly to its audiences, those that worship at the feet of Big Tech.

It won't surprise you to learn that Andreessen's strategy of front-running traditional journalism makes me uncomfortable as someone who values the fourth estate's role as a barometer of where society is headed. But the firm understands how the narrative battle is fought now: not always by convincing a small subset of critics of your point of view but by activating a larger group of advocates to overwhelm any noise those critics may be able to cause. They didn't invent these tactics; if anything, they are applying to industry communications the same approach that we on the Obama team applied to politics.

One could argue that it was Barack Obama who first perfected the use of digital media to circumvent traditional journalism to take a narrative straight to the masses, organizing advocates through social media and email especially. Whether it be Obama telling us stories about hope and collective power in the face of a cynical DC press corps, Trump turning the blame around on media stories of his own corruption, or private companies like Coinbase and Uber giving us information from their perspectives in the face of media criticism, the dispersion of media gatekeepers has both positive and negative effects on society, depending on the circumstances and depending on your own point of view. But for now, at least, this is the battlefield we've been given, and I believe we can't cede the ground to those who would use it to nefarious ends. If we won't engage in narrative building, someone else will.

Bringing Your People Along

Narrative building is key to changing public perception and bringing external audiences along on a journey toward making change together. But the tools of narrative building have focused for too long on external audiences at the expense of internal ones. Internal communications is often one of the most underappreciated parts of any change initiative even though when done right, employees can be some of a company's most powerful advocates.

I've seen way too many companies in my career prioritize a public relations spin about the company's social impact only to have employees, who have been empowered with their own digital mega-phones (despite what any company policy may say about the usage of social media), call bullshit because the company didn't properly put enough focus on cleaning up its internal house first.

Culture building externally and culture building internally work similarly. Employees need storytelling over time through multiple touchpoints to have a narrative about how the company is moving in the right direction take hold, especially if the story to date has been the opposite. Crisis management works similarly. If a story breaks internally, waves of anger from employees are likely to spill into the public arena and capture the attention of the press.

In recent years, several companies have underappreciated their company culture and made changes that angered their employees, who then took to social media to voice their frustrations. Return-ing to the example of Basecamp, its declaration of policy changes were announced proudly in a blog post by its founders without con-sideration for the direction its employees were headed. Employees of the company had been putting in the work to develop a commit-tee focused on diversity, equity, and inclusion. The new policy shut it down before it could get started. The disconnect between how Basecamp's leaders saw the company—and how they pictured them-selves as champions of work culture—and how employees viewed the company could have been bridged if Basecamp had spent at least as much time gathering feedback internally as it did making pronouncements externally. If external communication best prac-tices now require a series of microcampaigns and data gathering, we can do that with internal communications, too, finding small and large touchpoints with our employees to gut-check our culture and employee understanding of our direction.

Instead of having internal communications be solely the domain of human resources—or worse, completely distributed among company leaders, with no real centralized message—forward-thinking large companies are treating their internal communications with the same care and attention that they're treating their marketing. If employees can be your best advocates, employees should be considered a core audience.

At 18 Coffees, we've helped several clients set up internal teams dedicated to changing management with sophisticated communications capabilities, recognizing the importance of storytelling to your own people. Too many company leaders treat building a narrative about a major change as an afterthought—something to be checked off with one all-company memo from the CEO—instead of the war of attrition that it is, something requiring constant touchpoints, constant persuasion and realignment.

The need for building a narrative is greatest at different points in the change's life cycle, and understanding that life cycle is key to telling a story about change appropriately. Often when a big change is announced (assuming it is at all) there is internal excitement at first. Employees on the front lines are often the first to call for business transformation, recognizing the market need for operating differently because they're the closest to the market. But that excitement inevitably wanes over time as ambition meets reality and people begin to understand how the change will affect their jobs and their own internal priorities. This is when people's babies begin to be called ugly, and they can start to get defensive and overly protective of their team's output. From a timeline perspective, this is the trough of disillusionment. It's when persuasion matters the most but is often when employees hear the least about the success or failure of the change efforts. Rumors and disinformation often run rampant. Using consistent touchpoints matched with key moments of feedback and data gathering so that employees feel heard can help push through the trough as the change effort starts to pay off and eventually sees value.

One advantage that internal communications teams have over those focused on marketing externally is that there is a system already set up to organize direct communication to employees: the org chart. Company communications to employees that is paired with key messages delivered to them in their one-on-one meetings with their managers can be a powerful combination that helps reinforce the *why* behind the change and bring home the implications of the transformation for each employee's job. But it does require some internal organizing, not just handing down talking points to managers.

You have to recognize that top-down communication about a change effort is often met with as much skepticism from managers as it is from frontline employees. Managers should be engaged with and trained separately, and those with natural influence in the organization should be brought along as the change leaders and given real responsibility over its success.

In chapter six, we'll talk about how distributing responsibility and ownership over change, rather than centralizing it, ensures ownership of the change throughout the company. Senior leadership (including the board), middle management, and frontline employees should all be considered different audiences who need different key messages related to their different motivations and concerns.

Company leaders are often so focused on the external, trying to meet the demands of the changing market with bold transformation, that internal audiences become an afterthought. Imagine if sports teams did it that way: broadcasting plays externally without consulting with team members or lining up all their players to understand the objective of the play. When managed intentionally, employee engagement is one of the most powerful narrative-building tools a company has, and leaders should treat their employees as their secret weapon. If knowledge workers are like volunteers, who are engaged with companies at will and can take their knowledge elsewhere at any time, imagine if we organized them like that: people who want to give their time for a mission they believe in, ready and willing to be a part of changing the story of your company.

5

Better Takes Practice

Jack was struggling with transition, new expectations about his responsibilities, and defining his new role—which is not uncommon when you're five years old. Our son had a tough kindergarten year. We'd experienced his separation anxiety throughout preschool and were expecting some strong emotions about going to "big kid" school with his older brother. We weren't disappointed.

The first few weeks of kindergarten were fraught with screaming, tears, and outright refusing to go. Working with his teacher and the school counselor, we tried everything: giving him pep talks the night before and the morning of, slowly leaving the classroom so he could get used to being there, having the teacher pick him up in the hall so we didn't have to go in at all, his older brother (generously) walking him to class. We tried sticker charts and other motivational tools. Hell, we even tried outright bribery, promising toys and candy if only he would go without a fuss. After months of hard mornings, we were desperate.

When you're an exhausted parent, the temptation to shame your child into better behavior is a strong one. *Why can't you be more like your brother? He never had problems going to school.* When trying to get the kind of behavior you want, pointing out how destructive their current behavior can be, especially as compared to those around them, is sometimes a natural response. But any parenting expert will tell you that this tactic is counterproductive and can have long-term negative effects on the child's self-esteem. Shaming our child—especially since he had no control over how his body was reacting to his anxiety—would have been a fast track to hurting our relationship.

Being a parent has made me especially cognizant of how our minds work when faced with new circumstances and how different motivations and different emotions can affect our reactions to them. There's nothing like facing a new developmental stage with your child to not only test their behavior change abilities, but also to test your patience when dealing with intransigence. Immovable object, meet unstoppable force.

Ultimately, two things worked for changing his behavior. Time was the most important factor. But what helped us accelerate that timeline was a ritual he and I created for his mornings before class. The night before, I started making what I called bravery tokens with construction paper and stickers that I would debut with fanfare for him the next morning. The badges were nothing special, just something small he could carry around in his pocket to help him feel brave. But the ritual was the important part: giving him a new token every morning that he knew I'd made just for him helped break the cycle of the anxiety.

Change often happens like that. Jack wasn't a bad kid because he had a strong reaction to a new environment. His difficult behavior had nothing to do with his identity—but it would have if we had made the difficult behavior a part of his identity by the way we reacted. Ultimately, a new ritual helped him visualize a braver version of himself. Sometimes practicing at being better is all we need to become better.

At 18 Coffees, we've always said that organizations don't change—people change. And understanding how and why they change is the best way to ensure organizational success. In this chapter, we'll explore several nuances for how and why people change in response to new information, and why changing mindsets can be so hard. And importantly, we'll talk about how leaders scale individual mindset change in order to have a corporate impact.

Facts & Shame

On New Year's Eve 2020, the passengers of the PV Delice Party Cruise ran into trouble. Celebrating the New Year off the coast of Puerto Vallarta, the sixty passengers prepared to head back to land when the rear of the boat began taking on water. The captain sent out an SOS, and ten small boats in the area came to help. The entire scene was documented on social media by the partygoers themselves. They never expected to become famous. When images from the story were reshared on the Instagram account GaysOverCovid, the internet celebrated as if the ocean itself were shutting down a party that was putting people in danger.

GaysOverCovid and accounts like it developed massive follow-ings during the pandemic because of their use of schadenfreude as entertainment. Followers reveled in the misfortunes of those they felt were flouting health requirements, projecting anxieties about the pandemic onto strangers they felt deserved the ridicule. But shaming actually does little to change people's behavior. In fact, it's often counterproductive.

When we want someone to behave differently, we tend to unload what we perceive as logical arguments on them, trying to convince them of our way of thinking. But when people are presented with facts that go against the narrative they've already convinced them-selves is true, it can counterproductively reinforce that narrative, rather than tear it down.

We all have a set of beliefs that reinforce one another, a way of seeing the world unique to us, held together by what psychologists call coherence, meaning we see how all the pieces work together. An assault on those beliefs can cause a backfire effect because our core beliefs can be so critical to our identity. Instead of changing our minds, we search for any contrary evidence to the argument that confirms our existing beliefs, no matter how specious those argu-ments may be—and in the age of internet disinformation, many spe-cious arguments are readily available. Or, as in the case of responses to coronavirus mandates, we'll downplay our own behavior as not as bad as those around us and look for any whataboutisms that may justify the decision we've already made.

The fact is that facts are only so helpful when trying to change someone's behavior, especially if we don't have a strong relationship with that person. We live in a world of counterfactual arguments, and anyone desperate to confirm their own beliefs is able to find others in concert who also believe the same thing. Third-party validation of just about any belief is possible in a world of infinite information and alternative facts, and as we've already covered, journalistic gatekeepers only have so much credibility, depending on who the audience is.

In late 2020, a group of MIT scientists ran a Twitter experiment. They wanted to see whether or not presenting counterfactual arguments to those spreading political misinformation would help adjust the behavior of the spreader, leading to more informed opinions. Over the course of a year, they used a massive volunteer army to respond to specific political misinformation with notes suggesting that story had been debunked and links to articles to read more, becoming the embodiment of the online reply guy. More than a thousand people received their responses, and the researchers found that instead of correcting their behavior, the spreaders of misinformation actually *doubled down* on their behavior, becoming more stubborn than they were before. Political ideologies were so innate that no amount of debunking information would help.

When logic fails those of us trying to change minds, we often resort to shame. For example, when the scientific benefits of wearing a mask to prevent the spread of the coronavirus don't convince someone to do it, our natural instinct may be to stigmatize those who refuse. This is understandable from a public health standpoint because literal separation of the maskless and the masked is kind of the point, but it works in the opposite direction, too: in communities that had largely bought into anti-mask narratives, people were shamed or made fun of for wearing them. But unsurprisingly, this kind of public berating usually starts online in the comments on Facebook, in quote tweets, and in millions of screenshots shared around the internet daily screaming *look at this idiot*.

In actuality, shaming is more about us than it is about the target of the shame. When we become uncomfortable with those who choose behaviors that seem illogical, we lash out and look for refuge in the confirmation of others who also may be frustrated with that behavior. We tell ourselves that shaming people is an effective deterrent, but it's actually counterproductive. Shame attacks a person's sense of competence. Stigmatized people feel not only their behavior being questioned, but their very identity as well. Shame tells someone that they are bad, not just that their behavior may be bad. It challenges a person's identity in a way that makes them withdraw to protect themselves and—just like those of us who were doing the shaming—seek refuge in the confirmation of others, creating a vicious cycle of shaming and digging in heels. Stigmatized people feel pushed out of society, and that is a dangerous place for people to be.

It's important to note here the difference between *shame* and *guilt*, which is often highly dependent on the existing relationship between the two parties. If a foundation of trust has already been established, people will be more willing to listen to new information. Guilt allows the person receiving the new information to focus on their behavior, not their identity as a bad person. Shaming can be extremely manipulative if abused in the context of an existing relationship. We don't want to stigmatize those we care about, but often that is the outcome of shaming tactics.

In general, we have to recognize our own motivations for wanting people to change. Often we approach arguments from the context of unilateral control, meaning the only outcome that is acceptable is full commitment to our point of view. I'm right, you're wrong, and there is no in-between. This is a recipe for relational disaster and, for our purposes, stationary mindsets, as opposed to growth mindsets that are open to new perspectives and ways of being. We have to recognize that just as we have our identities tied up in our perspectives, those we're arguing with also see themselves in their beliefs, and there are self-presentational psychological consequences for admitting they're wrong.

There is no societal change or organizational change without individual change, and individual change doesn't happen when people are stuck in their own ideological corners. I'm not asking that you unilaterally disarm or give up on your own beliefs or your own facts, but I am asking that you seek an alternative to unilateral control, shaming, or calling out.

Conversion & Coherence

Thank God for 9/11 and God Hates Fags are relatively known messages displayed on the signs of the hate group Westboro Baptist Church while protesting American soldiers' funerals in the US. The group's virulent anti-LGBTQ and anti-Jewish tactics are known and accepted by the congregation's members, and for a long time, Megan Phelps-Roper, granddaughter of the church's founder, was no exception. Then one day, Phelps-Roper walked away from the church and its hateful ideology. What drove her decision to leave something she had believed in her entire life?

Operating as the social media director for WBC, her about-face began with Twitter. Initially used as a tool to spread the church's hateful propaganda, Phelps-Roper's beliefs began to change when confronted with thoughtful messages from people who disagreed with the church's stances. David Abitbol, an influential Jewish voice on Twitter, engaged with her ideas instead of mocking her outright. Eventually, he won her over. (The two are now married.)

Phelps-Roper transformed from a leader of a hate group to an activist fighting to overcome divisions between religious and political groups. With her new coherence came a new mission: to help those who were like her break out of their mental routines and see the world a different way. Her extreme example is one of the kinds of small conversions that happen all the time.

We engage every day with thousands of persuasion messages. The marketplace of ideas has become infinitely deep and oftentimes extremely narrow. The ideas we consume are decided by some combination of choice and the algorithms we keep. But the potential for conversion exists more than ever before.

It's hard for us to listen when we know in our bones that someone else is wrong. It's even harder when they're wrong in a way that is offensive or causes harm. But there are proven models that show how listening, even to those who we could easily see as lost, even when their beliefs are offensive to our very existence, is still a powerful strategy for persuasion and behavior change. It makes sense when we consider ourselves in the other person's seat. We'd be the first to call foul if we didn't think the other person was listening to our point of view.

If we think about a person's belief system as made of a coherent set of ideas that make their worldview possible, then persuasion works best when it gradually unwinds those ideas, sowing incoherence where once there was certainty. This is where the war of attrition that is narrative building becomes personal. When we combine repeated exposure to new ideas with personal connection and demonstrated empathy, knots that were once tied strongly in the mind begin to loosen.

A *come-to-Jesus moment* is a popular phrase in American culture. It describes a dramatic conversion event, when someone becomes enlightened about a new point of view and realizes the error of their past beliefs, not unlike the dramatic tent revivals of American evangelical Christianity. We apply this idiom to all kinds of mind changes, but it betrays our hope that behavior change can be an overnight conversion, when, in fact, changing minds most often happens in gradual stages, as it did for Phelps-Roper. It requires consistent listening, engagement, and a lot of patience.

Ultimately, when we're asking someone to change their core beliefs and their behavior, we're asking them to change their identity. In fact, I would argue that with the massive amount of persuasive messaging we're presented with in our digitally connected lives every day, identity has become territory we stake out in order not to get lost in the digital infinite. Identifying with groups that seem like us, people who share our interests and beliefs, has become safe harbor in the chaos of everyday life. We choose to carve out our own part of the world with our own people, which includes the rituals, ideology, and perceived enemies of those people, because without those associations, life in the infinite is too hard to bear. Identity groups help us navigate what should matter to us and when.

Part of why coherence is so powerful is that it creates a story about the world and gives us our place in it. If that world isn't the world we thought it was, where do we belong? Not having an answer to that question is a scary place to be, which is one of the reasons C. T. Vivian was so adamant in his work about having a place for ex-KKK members to land. Part of changing someone's mind is to give them a new coherence, new rituals, and, sometimes, new perceived enemies. Identity transformation is a scary concept for us to wrap our heads around, but we often do it unknowingly. Since we're works in progress who believe we're finished, sometimes our transition to new thinking happens unconsciously.

Social Constructs & Degenerative Behavior

When I moved to the Chicago suburbs from the city, I was excited to have a wide-open space for my kids to play in—until a few months in when I realized how much work lawn maintenance actually requires. Having a lush lawn that makes you and your neighbors happy requires constant watering, fertilizing, cutting, and reseeding; otherwise, your yard quickly becomes patchy, discolored, and overrun by weeds. There is no status quo when it comes to a yard. It's either getting better or it's getting worse. (We eventually moved back to the city, where we now keep a tiny but beautiful urban garden.)

I like to think organizational behavior is like lawn maintenance: it takes pruning, of course, but it also takes fertilization and seeding the right kinds of behavior to encourage it to take root. And much like a lawn, there is no status quo. Without attention, negative cultural ideas and behaviors will grow like weeds. Too many weeds and the healthy grass will be overrun.

An organization is made up of individual people making individual decisions that together decide the fate of the company. Organizations at their core are, after all, social constructs: the policies, workflows, and even hierarchy and reporting structures all function because *we agree they should*, not because an org chart is something that exists in objective reality. Collectively, we give policy its power, and violation of policy its consequences. It's easy to feel as if we exist in a machine and that we sometimes get ground up in that machine's moving parts. But viewing an organization as a social construct can both reduce that machine's mental hold over us and point us to solutions for behavior change that are ultimately more about mindset and organizational behavior than they are about project management. Ultimately, the only way organizations as constructs change is if the people collectively change.

People are capable of deluding themselves and spreading that delusion to others. Organizational defensive routines occur when we've collectively put boundaries around what we believe we are capable of or not capable of. When we say things like "that could never happen here," what we're really saying is that we've convinced ourselves through cultural ritual that there are limits to what our organization can pull off.

I saw this in politics all the time. Political parties are the ultimate social constructs because they have a limited hierarchy, despite all the press about how parties are moving in one direction or another. Because parties are ideologically driven, especially in the US, there is constant infighting over party direction and policy, and disappointment when the party fails to achieve its goals. That leads to "Dems in disarray" narratives within the Democratic Party and "Republicans in name only" name-calling within the Republican Party. The party faithful begin to slip into cynicism, and suddenly the common refrain is what little the party is able to achieve.

The greatest revered leaders of both parties in recent decades, like Ronald Reagan and Barack Obama, were able to break the defensive routines by appealing to a higher purpose and demonstrating what they believed the country and the party would be capable of if we worked together.

Politics is not the only arena in which we self-sabotage while blaming the other side. Our workplace is made up of the same kinds of conflicts, sometimes malicious but often unintentional. In Peter Senge's classic work on systems behavior, *The Fifth Discipline,* Senge outlines a concept called accidental adversaries, a system archetype that describes when people in an organization find themselves at odds even while cooperating toward a common goal because they've accidentally taken actions to undermine each other's success.

For example, as the leader of the marketing department, I may not have given Joanna's work in IT a second thought until Joanna's goal of information security conflicted with my team's goal of experimenting with new social media management platforms. Suddenly we found ourselves at odds, arguing in leadership meetings over goals that feel binary, though we both have the organization's best interest in mind. We became accidental adversaries when our behavior degenerated over time.

Personal conflicts like this can get stuck in negative feedback loops like those illustrated below, where anticipating our adversary's next moves causes us to act defensively, which the other person interprets as aggression and responds to by acting defensively as well. Breaking the cycle takes a certain amount of emotional intelligence or direct intervention by leaders willing to chaperone a tête-à-tête, where both parties can review their behavior and each other's motivations, and realign toward mutual success.

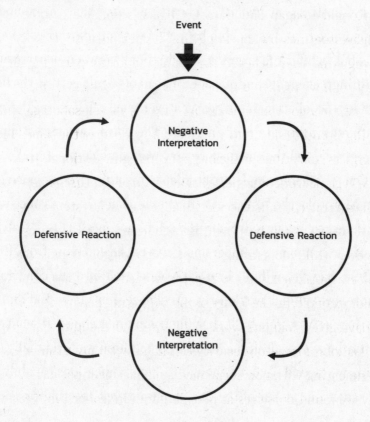

Event

Negative Interpretation

Defensive Reaction

Defensive Reaction

Negative Interpretation

Adversarial relationships have often been cultivated by management in order to inspire competition between departments and offices. Friendly competition by itself is not a bad thing, but often leaders build competition into their organization's workflow and structure without an appreciation of the unintended consequences or a balance of weight on interdepartmental cooperation.

When I worked at a major marketing agency, for example, each department operated under separate profit and loss (P&L) statements, a policy meant to spur on competition and innovation among corporate, digital, consumer marketing, and other practice areas at the time. In reality, instead of each practice area finding its own lines of business, many shared clients, meaning that the competition management was seeking happened not outside of the agency's walls but behind the scenes in negotiations between departments regarding a client's scope of work. Instead of clients getting the best team for the job, they often got whatever team a VP in one department could negotiate over another. (The office has since stopped the practice, and the entire office now works under one P&L.)

One famous example of interdepartmental adversaries comes from Motorola, the famous electronics company that was once well positioned to be out in front of the cell phone market. Bob Galvin, son of the company's founder and CEO of the company from 1959 to 1990, had firmly built internal competition into the company's culture, believing it would drive excellence. For many years it did just that, as Motorola built thriving communications and semiconductors businesses. But the internal competition was eventually the company's downfall. Even though its communications capabilities had put it out ahead of the cell phone market, internal divisions kept the culture from capitalizing on the growing industry, as the heads of the network technology and handset technology divisions refused to work cooperatively.

The idea that competition drives excellence is as old as capitalism itself, and, for better or worse, is endemic to our economy and much of our corporate culture. I believe competition itself is not a bad thing, but unchecked it can become like those few weeds that destroy your lawn. The winners suck up all the nutrients, leaving no oxygen or fresh water for anyone else. Change leadership means viewing the organization as a sum of its parts, even as the parts make individual decisions.

Small Steps

I've worked with many nonprofits over the years, and we've often talked about an idea called the theory of change that is foundational to why the nonprofit does its work and how it gets its donors and volunteers involved. The basic idea is to answer the questions Why does what we do now matter in the long run? And how can this small action I'm taking today contribute to the larger mission of the organization?

The theory of change ties each contribution back to how we're going to make a difference together. At Organizing for Action (OFA), for example, we thought about our theory of change every time we asked someone to give five dollars, sign a petition, or call their senators. We tried to make a persuasive case that what they were doing mattered. For instance, if enough of us call our senator to encourage them to vote the way we want on a piece of legislation, it will pass the Senate.

This is an idea that deserves more airtime in the rest of the economy, not just in nonprofits. Why should buying your product matter? What kind of mission is your company looking to achieve, and do I want my wallet contributing to that mission? (Is it more than just making money?)

The theory of change really matters when an organization is going through a transformation. Each employee needs to understand their role in making the change—not just passively how the change will affect them, but why their contribution is actively needed to make the change a success.

A 2016 study from the consulting firm McKinsey & Company found that frontline engagement in a change effort really matters to its success: of those with successful transformations (as defined by improvement in an organization's performance in both the short and long terms), 73 percent reported frontline workers as visibly engaged. Among company transformations that failed to engage frontline workers, only 3 percent reported success. Remember, your employees are volunteers. They need to understand your theory of change more than any other stakeholder so they can find their place in it. Employees who understand their role in making changes are more likely to buy into the success of the organization and are less afraid of the consequences of the change on their specific roles.

I've often seen leaders create grand strategic visions for where their company should go—usually loaded with buzzwords and industry clichés, which makes management very proud of itself but only confuses those actually doing the work. Change has to be tangible in order to be actionable. Our team at 18 Coffees has often counseled leaders to make a transformation initiative as tangible as the Cookie

Monster's end goal. No one questions what the Cookie Monster wants at the end of the day: cookies. The end goal of a transformation needs to be visceral and appealing on an emotional level.

In order to achieve successful involvement from the entire organization, change has to be broken down into manageable and measurable steps. It's important here to differentiate between *technical change* and *adaptive change*. Technical change is about which new systems are going to be implemented and which old ones are going to be shuttered. It's the most linear part of any change initiative because it has a definitive stopping point—unfreeze, change, refreeze. New technologies, new processes, new systems may need to be constantly optimized, but at some point the work switches from implementation to optimization, and the transformation for all intents and purposes is complete. Technical change can be broken down into an infinite number of exhaustive steps (I've seen transformation work plans with enough minutiae to cause eyestrain), and each step can be assigned to owners throughout the organization, distributing responsibility for success.

Technical Change	Adaptive Change
Clearly defined end goal	Ongoing
Clear expertise needed	Tackling cultural challenges
Can be reduced to specific steps and tasks	Focused on behavior change

Adaptive change is the harder, more human part of change management because it involves our behavior and because it has no point B. If organizations are social constructs, then transformations only function correctly because our behavior has changed accordingly. The best systems are subject to human error at best, and human neglect at worst. That's why when we counsel our clients on a transformation, our most important key performance indicators are not about technical change; they're about behavior. We want to look at how a culture is being changed by how its people are acting differently. If a sales team, for example, has identified that moving from one customer relationship management platform (CRM) to another will ultimately help it reach its sales goals, the implementation of that new technology solution would not be enough to declare success. Ultimately, leaders need to know that sales reps are consistently using the new solution as intended. If they aren't, then the leaders need to identify why and make adjustments.

Adaptive behavior change often needs reinforcement along the way in order to transform a culture that was set in its ways. Nudge theory, the idea that positive behavior can be encouraged through small reinforcements, is a relatively new field of behavioral economics that has had radical implications for health and wellness outcomes in the private sector (my Apple Watch, for example, just nudged me to stand instead of sit, writing this page for more than an hour). The theory is just starting to be applied in interesting ways to the workplace. Employers who need to remind workers to operate in different ways, such as to knowledge-share on internal message boards to break down silos, or encourage their inclusion of team members with different perspectives, have started experimenting with emails, text messages, and other ways to nudge employees at key moments to remember their commitments to different behavior. Some of those platforms have also become excellent sources of data collection, not just on the application of new behaviors, but also on employee clarity or satisfaction when going through a change.

Companies are complex organisms composed of employees with various levels of confidence and clarity on any change initiative. The more you can get them involved in a change from the beginning, the more you keep in touch with them along the way and remind them of shared goals, the better the change outcomes will be. If narrative is a war of attrition, behavior change can be its collateral damage. When you lose touch with how your employees are acting and reacting to a change initiative, you risk winning a battle but losing the war.

Rituals for Change

New rituals around changed behavior are powerful because of their ability to scale. To an individual, rituals serve as a powerful reminder about the transformation they are undergoing. But to a community, rituals become the practice of transformation itself. We do things differently on purpose because we are aiming to become better together. When I incorporate the ritual of sharing my pronouns, for example, I remind others to do the same, and together we aim to be more inclusive of the transgender and nonbinary colleagues among us. Rituals are the intersection of ambition and practice, and they are the connective tissue between individual change and corporate change.

A good ritual bonds teams together in big and small ways, whether or not they are connected directly to the work. My wife is big on creating rituals for our family in order to give our children repeatable memories. As a teacher, she shares the same summer break as our kids. To kick each one off, our family does a fun activity together to mark the end of the school year and the beginning of the summer. Then at the end of the summer, we do the opposite to celebrate the end of summer and the beginning of a new school year. The activities have varied from going to a theme park to seeing a baseball game to just going somewhere special to get everyone's favorite kind of ice cream. But they're a deviation from our family's norm in a way that is memorable, and our kids always look forward to them.

Good teams are intentional about building in these kinds of experiences. On the Obama team, we had a ritual of celebrating our teammates when they took a vacation by doing something completely ridiculous to their workstations. I'll never forget the day I came back to my desk to find it covered in images of Justin Bieber (our Twitter nemesis due to his account being one of the only accounts with more followers than Barack Obama at the time).

We also used rituals to discourage behavior. Because we worked in politics, information security was a paramount concern. Whenever a coworker walked away from their computer without first locking their screen, someone inevitably sent a message from their email account to all their coworkers with some embarrassing (but playful) message. Rituals can be powerful for shaping culture.

Zipcar was one of the first ride-sharing services in the US, but over time, it found itself facing market pressure. The company had designed its entire customer experience to be web based and accessed through a desktop or laptop computer. New competitors like Uber and Lyft had built completely mobile experiences designed to go with the customer in the ride. Zipcar realized that in order to innovate, it needed to change its corporate culture by drawing a memorable line in the sand with its employees.

To emphasize how the company was shifting to a mobile-first mindset, employees were invited to a meeting where leadership discussed the new direction. To help stress the point, leadership passed around sledgehammers and invited each employee to smash two desktop computers. The dramatic experience of symbolically destroying the old way of working created a lasting impression on the staff and became part of the internal story of the new direction. Importantly, the one-time drama was then reinforced through other rituals, like regular customer roundtables, where employees could hear directly from mobile-first millennials.

Much has been written about the power of small daily habits to change people's lives. (The only way I could write this book while running my company was to consistently write first thing in the morning for several months.) The key to building healthy habits is to start with a few manageable rituals and build on them over time. If I don't regularly exercise, suddenly adding two-a-days to try to transform my body overnight is a recipe for burnout at best, or injury at worst. Often people have to start with making their healthy habits just a little easier or their bad habits just a little harder—such as following the twenty-second rule coined by positive psychologist Shawn Achor, which is about tricking your brain into different behaviors by adding only twenty seconds of friction in front of an undesirable behavior.

The nonprofit and political organizing worlds use the phrase *ladder of engagement* to describe the pursuit of behavior change.

At its core, the ladder of engagement is about deepening engagement with a campaign over time. On the Obama team, we may have asked you to pay attention to an issue before asking you to indicate you cared about it, before asking you to commit time or money to fixing it. Each campaign was designed differently with different actions, but the point was that each ask created permission for the next one. At 18 Coffees, we've since applied this kind of organizer thinking to creating internal culture change.

Ladder of Engagement

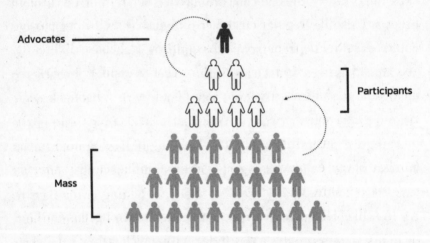

When working on a large-scale transformation effort, one of the most important things we measure is behavior change through a series of cascading rituals that grow over time. For a large telecommunications client looking to reinvent its product development process, we first focused on answering a few key questions for each product to slow down the process and add some intentionality to it. We applied a framework to the design process and measured how often designers used it. Then we added the ritual of community feedback in order for the organization to gut check itself against its own expectations. Over time, we were able to transform the go-to-market process through substantial culture change, using one new ritual at a time.

It's About the Mission

A complex organization moving from the status quo to something better is in a struggle for its identity, and its employees will experience a cognitive dissonance as it moves forward. How leaders manage that dissonance determines how much a cultural change will take hold. People have to be taught how to behave differently, and then they have to be rewarded for that new behavior. But it's important that they know even this new way of working may be critiqued and revised in the future. That's the difficulty of modern management: just when a new process may be taking hold in the mindset of our employees, some disruptive influence may force us to revise our thinking again.

Just like Hiebert's centered-set model, a strong mission and theory of change provide a north star with which to navigate when times get hard. But our people need to be brought along. Everyone being on a vector toward something meaningful together is more important than each milestone we reach along the way. Each will have its own significance, especially the demonstration of progress toward our shared mission, but a constant process is better. As long as we're aimed in the right direction, we have to be OK with the goalposts shifting on us.

The people we lead are likely to struggle with change fatigue at some point. The significance of our mission has to matter to keep people going. Negative reinforcement—like the threat of losing a job—isn't enough to create cultural momentum and can backfire on leaders by creating undercurrents of cynicism. People have to believe in the mission in order to make an effort, and the mission has to be constantly reinforced by leadership. The journey toward better is not about any one milestone. It's about the larger idea of where we're going together.

Having a mission that means something is also a buffer against changing people's behaviors for the wrong reasons. Critics of nudge theory believe it to be manipulative, arguing that small suggestions and reminders are meant as a backdoor to getting more productive output from employees at their expense. Any effort toward behavior change may slide into psychological engineering if not carefully considered and managed, but having a mission that's about something more than profit will at least give you a more solid ethical foundation for asking people to behave differently. When we're all rowing in the same direction toward something better, it becomes incumbent upon each of us to take up an oar and do our part.

Being better takes practice, and you as a leader have to be the first one to demonstrate how you're practicing. Any transformation that asks your people to change their behavior while you stay the same will ring hollow no matter how far removed from the actual technical change you might be. You have to demonstrate your commitment to the mission through shared sacrifice. If your people are going to learn to run, you have to be the one that teaches them to get on their feet and take the first step.

6

Build a Coalition for Change

When I met Connor, he was in the process of transforming his entire company. But he started out just wanting to make it a little less racist.

During the George Floyd protests in the summer of 2020, many corporations made promises about how they would treat their employees of color, especially their Black employees. Connor's company was no different. Connor felt that, as one of the largest telecommunications companies in the world, his organization had a real stake in creating an anti-racist business environment not only for his company's employees, but also for its customers. He quickly joined an internal task force dedicated to diversity, equity, and inclusion, where the implications of the George Floyd protests were a hot topic.

Months went by with little action, and Connor realized that the volunteer committee wasn't going to be well equipped to truly tackle issues of inclusion and anti-racism within such a complex enterprise. He and others also realized that the ethical issues the organization faced went beyond inclusion to how it thought about sustainability, accessibility, machine learning, user experience, and other interconnected issues that could potentially create moral hazard for the company. As a user-experience designer for digital products, Connor was on the front lines of seeing how these issues merged to create a complex web of problems for the company's most vulnerable customers.

Connor went to his leadership team and the chief technology officer for the company, who quickly bought in (to their credit) to a larger change initiative with some real resources behind it. But they didn't stop there. They knew that any successful ambitious effort to operationalize ethical thinking into how they developed and deployed products would need the buy-in of the heads of several departments, including technology, design, communications, and marketing. Connor went to work building a coalition of multiple representatives of each department, and together they engaged in a process that eventually resulted in them hiring 18 Coffees to work with them on transforming their culture.

Over the course of the engagement, we worked with their design, technology, and marketing teams to create an ethical north star that guided a redesign of their go-to-market process that quickly started having a more positive effect on community outcomes. Importantly, we worked with the leaders of their guiding coalition to merchandise this work internally, to make sure the culture shifted with the new way of working. We designated champions of the change, influential company leaders—outside of the org chart—who convinced their peers this was the right direction.

Connor's company isn't perfect—no enterprise working at its scale ever can be. But it has made real progress toward developing an adaptive change capability that allows them to constantly challenge themselves to look at different ethical issues regarding their work, all because leadership was willing to work with influencers within the company passionate about making change.

Constituencies and Coalitions

In 2012, a group of volunteers decided, without any kind of official permission, to overhaul the biggest employer in Europe.

Helen Bevan was working for the Institute for Innovation and Improvement, an internal consultancy for Britain's National Health Service, when she came across a group of trainee doctors who were frustrated about the NHS's stifling bureaucracy. Specifically, the group believed that the demands of the bureaucracy were keeping frontline health care workers from effective patient care. So Bevan's team decided to do something about it. It wasn't going to be easy. Conservative politician Nigel Lawson once described the NHS as "the closest thing the English people have to a religion." In addition to its being one of the world's largest employers, millions of people depended on the NHS—by some estimates the NHS dealt with over 1 million patients every thirty-six hours.

The team came up with the idea of inviting everyone across the NHS to identify what they personally could change to improve patient care without needing anyone else's permission and pledge to take that action themselves. Helen led the way as the team committed volunteer time to building a pledge portal that asked for individual or team contributions, including a call to action to share the website with others. The Change Day site went live in January 2013.

Through a dedicated campaign that included posting on internal communication channels and social media, sending out internal email appeals, and critically identifying internal influencers who could evangelize the Change Day effort, the pledges grew from 5,000 on February 14 to more than 189,000 pledges by the end of the campaign—50,000 of which came in on the last day. Change Day reframed change as a bottom-up effort, something where each contributor could reasonably have a positive impact. As one nurse stated, "Change Day made me realize that I have the power."

The next year, Change Day received more than 800,000 pledges. The following year, teams pioneered experiments with entirely new protocols. The success of Change Day proved a model that was repeated in nineteen other countries.

The Change Day experiment helped Helen Bevan realize the benefits of collective agency in a large bureaucracy, where individual initiative can easily be stifled. Large, complex organizations need structure, but changing them often works better when the agency can be decentralized, with individual leaders who feel empowered to do something about what they see around them that is broken. In fact, I'd argue that this is the only way systemic change happens.

Marshall Ganz, a lifelong organizer, academic, and one of the chief architects of the political organizing model of the 2008 Barack Obama presidential campaign, is credited as defining organizing as "leadership that enables people to turn the resources they have into the power they need to make the change they want." Ganz pioneered an approach to campaigns that emphasized the interconnectivity of the people involved in the political process of making change, as opposed to the old top-down approach to political decision-making.

Because of my background in political organizing, I can't help but see the parallels between how political campaigns empower individuals to use their collective power to make change, and how we have to organize our people in the workplace to make change. As I've already mentioned, when those who are most affected by the work get involved in making the change, beautiful things happen: the change actually takes hold because everyone has bought into its success.

The idea seems simple but actually carries with it added complexity because of the hierarchical nature of most organizations. Like political campaigns before Ganz's, large companies are still management heavy, focused on resource mobilization and opportunism instead of collective determination. And just like in politics, the powerful in hierarchies have constituencies whom they have to please. But unlike in politics, we may not always have a clear view into who those constituencies are. Interests don't always align cleanly with departments or org charts.

Leaders in organizations have a multilayered web of stakeholders whom they have to please with each decision, and often those stakeholders are at odds with each other over the company's direction. A head of product development may want to move aggressively with in-market testing of new products, while the head of finance feels like it's a waste of money and company resources. A marketing leader could be pushing the company to be more aggressive in responding to social issues, while the head of legal cautions against it. Understanding an organization as a web of constituencies with corresponding influences helps us map the power dynamics that are important while trying to make change, and appreciate why an organizing-centric approach can make such a difference in any change initiative's success.

Organizers try to understand power as influence at the intersection of competing interests—they even use exercises like power mapping to help them visually understand where those competing interests lie and where resources could be marshaled to influence the influencers. We've talked about organizations as complex systems, but ultimately, the people within them are systems unto themselves. They make rational and sometimes irrational decisions based on a mixture of self-interest and a commitment to organizational excellence, however they perceive it. Some intentionality around understanding those competing interests goes a long way to making sure influence is exerted in the direction you think it should be.

Basic Power Map Example

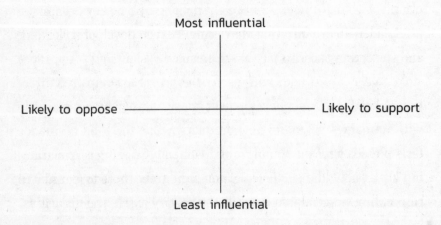

Workplace politics is often thought of in the negative, used as a derogatory phrase for the gossiping and infighting that happens at large organizations. But ultimately, politics is about strategy. You have to understand how people work and how influence is exerted across your organization if any initiative you care about is ever going to be successful. Presenting a rational case for change may feel like it should be enough to convince those above you to move in the right direction, but others may be presenting an equally rational case for the opposite. Understand the playing field, understand the players, and you're in a much better position to make change.

In order for a change to happen within a large, complex organization, it's ultimately going to take the alignment of all of those political interests in a coalition dedicated to resolving some kind of strategic dissonance. Coalitions don't have to be permanent and their members don't have to always agree on everything. But they can recognize a larger threat when they see it and deploy resources (time, talent, and budget) accordingly.

Recognizing that internal politics requires an organizing approach, we can start to apply the principles and practices of building effective coalitions to mobilize for change. Some key organizing practices we'll explore include telling stories, developing leaders, and structuring successful change teams.

The Three Stories

One of the key tenets of Ganz's approach to organizing is something he called public narrative. He claimed there are three essential stories each organizer needs to master: the story of self, the story of us, and the story of now. We can use the same organizing framework in considering how to mobilize our workforce. Let's start with the story most organizations want to tell: the story of now.

We've talked at length about how urgent change is for every organization and how I believe change leadership needs to become a core competency. But even if you still have trouble wrapping your mind around that, you can find a reason your organization needs to change right now if you look hard enough. Your sales process might be too slow. Your technology may be outdated; you may need to become more digital. Or there may be a new opportunity, innovation, or business model just over the horizon that will need something different from your people than your current model does. Whatever your situation, creating internal will requires you to lay out your case for the urgency of the moment—why this change needs to happen now. In his classic work *Managing at the Speed of Change*, Daryl Conner referred to this urgency as a "burning platform," an analogy that means the ground beneath you is disappearing and you have to evolve accordingly. (The problem now, of course, is that our platforms are always burning.)

Zipcar's sledgehammers became a part of their internal folklore, a grounding fable in their story. Other companies have acted with similar urgency and fanfare. In 2007, when Amazon introduced the original Kindle, leaders at Barnes & Noble saw the introduction of the device from such a growing competitor as an existential threat and rallied their internal teams around the creation of the Nook, which debuted only two years later.

In theory, with some effort, every organization should be able to create a story of now that is compelling enough to ground a change initiative. Creating a compelling story of us is much harder to develop, mostly because you immediately run into some combination of management distrust and organizational cynicism. The defensive routines we talked about in the last chapter can be compelling and are often activated immediately when someone starts talking about change. Ideally, work on both distrust and cynicism happens outside of a major change initiative—trust is built before you need to trade on it. But given the urgency and frequency of change, and the pace of turnover at the top, leaders are often forced into a situation where they have to do the best with what they have.

Much as it was with the Obama 2008 campaign, ultimately a successful story of us is grounded in hope. When Helen Bevan's team asked people to commit to small steps to change the NHS, it was asking them to believe in the power of collective action to transform such an important organization. When our telecom client rallied its internal coalitions to rethink their product development process, they were asking each other to believe such a massive enterprise could have a positive impact in local communities. When we ask people to believe in what an organization is capable of, we're asking them to take a risk regarding their livelihood—and we're asking them to believe in themselves.

Which brings us to the final story: the story of self. This story is the most important tool in an organizer's toolbox because it relates the change back to something personal for the individual. Your own story explains how you arrived at leadership in the first place. What was it that made you want to be in the position you're in? What choices did you make along the way that inform who you are as a person, as a professional? And how did that position give you a special place of significance to see why this change needs to happen now? Elements of my own story, for example, include being a parent, having family history of mental illness, and being an entrepreneur. Those are three parts of my story that I frequently rely on when talking to other business leaders about employee care.

When we combine all three stories, we have a powerful narrative for bringing people along on a change initiative. Stories appeal to people's emotional centers, not just their rational brains, allowing for more opportunities for persuasion. When people understand the bigger picture and their place in it, they are more likely to come along willingly. Stories create a sense of shared purpose through the power of vulnerability: when I share my history and my motivations for wanting something to be different, it creates permission for you to do the same. When you feel like you are in the trenches with someone, powerful bonds are formed.

Centralization and Power

As a senior executive of a company, you have unique insight into your organization. Because you sit atop the org chart, you are able to see problems from a viewpoint most in your organization won't have—and you especially should be able to see the interconnected nature of the organization in a way that helps you determine strategy. As a business leader myself, I understand the unique insight management roles can and should contain, and how that responsibility often brings with it the instinct to make sure you're involved in every important decision. That style of management may have worked when the world moved more slowly, but now that kind of centralization often works to bottleneck important change initiatives, making a company much less adaptable.

In many complex organizations, centralization often kills change momentum. Employees bring issues to management, but ultimately, management is the only one in the building with the power to initiate change. And by the time the CEO becomes aware of an issue important enough to marshal resources to move in a new direction, it's usually too late. The organization is turning in one direction while the market has already turned in another.

Centralization itself as a concept has become antithetical to the modern distributed world. One of Silicon Valley's favorite clichés is to talk about how a new technology has democratized something: social media has democratized communications, cryptocurrency has democratized money, etc. But within the cliché is a truism about our expectation of individual participation. In a connected world, when we are one of the nodes in a moving system, we expect to have a voice. The hierarchy of most management structures in this environment feels antiquated and oppressive.

Titles have their limits when it comes to influencing the success of a transformation. We've already talked about how important it is to get the front line involved in a change initiative's success, but research by Dr. Leandro Herrero has also shown the limits of hierarchical power. In a 2014 study of change initiatives within European companies, he showed that people who are highly connected within an organization have twice as much power to influence change as people with hierarchical power. Organizers understand that community power trumps titles every time.

Leadership has an important role in complex systems because every decision made in one part of the system may affect other parts or may change the system as a whole. Someone needs to keep their eye on the interrelated nature of organizations, and that responsibility naturally falls to the people who can see the moving parts from the highest vantage point. Scientists talk about emergent properties of complex systems being values that the entire system has, but each part of the system is lacking. Think of your organization like a film, with each department being a still image in that film. When all the pieces work together, motion is created—an emergent property of the film that no individual image can reproduce. Someone has to see what the movie is like when it's all put together and being projected.

But too often leaders come at this awesome responsibility with their egos on full display. It makes sense when you think about how people in power got to be in power in the first place: through competition and self-interest. Whatever the purity of their motives for seeking out leadership positions, ultimately managers had to play the bureaucratic game of one-upmanship to get where they are today and be rewarded with power they are often reluctant to give up.

In order to move at the speed of a digital world, you as a leader will need to cede some level of control. We've already talked about how successful change initiatives are when frontline workers are involved in its direction, almost three times as successful as top-down initiatives. But the power to initiate a change also has to come from more than just you. Adaptive organizations that move at the speed of digital have a shared sense of responsibility throughout the organization—and an evolutionary instinct that gives them a high capacity for staying relevant.

Developing Change Leaders

All movements gain power through their commitment to develop leadership, which makes building up new leaders one of the core principles of good organizing. In the Obama model, leadership development was a core tenet of how communities were organized. Certain volunteers were identified for their leadership capacity, were trained to become community leaders, and then went on to train and organize others. This snowflake model, as it was called, extended the reach and influence of the campaign's paid staff and distributed responsibility for the campaign's success, creating an interdependency that reflected the shared goals of the campaign. Intentional relationship building and leadership coaching in this way is a cornerstone of collective power, and essential to mobilizing internal coalitions that can push an organization forward.

Influence is a fickle thing within the walls of any organization. Sometimes it's wielded by those with official power to make decisions, and sometimes those whispering in the ears of the most powerful decision makers are just as powerful. Developing leaders who can navigate the political dynamics of an organization means that a change team has distributed influence throughout your organization. Those leaders understand the levers of power in different departments and can use the three stories to bring the culture of that department along with the change. But those leaders also need the ability to make independent decisions, to scope out and initiate microchange initiatives of their own.

If the centralization of all major decision-making is a surefire way to kill change momentum, then leaders throughout the organization need to be given pathways for flagging systems that are broken, new opportunities in the market, and ways the organization could potentially be disrupted. Then they need the individual authority to be able to make that change happen. Collectively, the system needs to be able to self-heal. Senior executives who exercise too much power over deciding what needs to change will find themselves leading an organization on the brink of irrelevance with frustrated and cynical employees. Leadership development means strategically deploying trust that your people are capable of navigating tough decisions.

Key Change Leadership Skills
• Able to navigate internal politics
• Flexible and adaptable to new situations
• Able to balance individual authority and community decision-making
• Knows when to strategically initiate conflict

Leaders of change recognize the need to strategically initiate conflict, creating dissonance between the status quo and any number of possible new realities. Sometimes that means inviting competing internal factions to a shared table in order to hash out existing conflicts. Sometimes it means introducing a new idea into a relatively stable work environment in order to shake it out of complacency. And sometimes it means creating internal conflict within people who've become too comfortable in their roles. Some companies actively build conflict and conflict resolution into their corporate culture. Intel is famous for its constructive confrontation model instituted under CEO Andy Grove in the late 1990s. Or take Johnson & Johnson, whose leaders proactively extract lessons from conflict in order to extract strategic value from areas of disagreement.

The role of a manager is to create order out of chaos, whereas the role of a leader is to create chaos out of order. Leaders shake up the status quo by pushing their organizations into new horizons. Managers make sure the chaos created by good leadership doesn't devolve into disorder and a lack of productivity. This duality often gives all the glory to leaders while managers get a bad rap for being bureaucratic buzzkills, but the truth is that both skills are needed and, importantly, both can be practiced.

When we talk about leadership development, we're actually talking about developing both kinds of skills. Leaders appeal to the emotional core of an argument and are able to rally constituencies around a shared purpose using the stories mentioned earlier. Managers control the technical aspects of a movement for change to make sure the change actually happens, managing work plans, Gantt charts, communications, and deliverables. We've all at one point had to be an effective leader or an effective manager despite our job titles or authority. Effective change teams include people mastered in both, even if they lean toward one end of the spectrum or the other. We'll explore these two dimensions of leadership more in chapter nine.

Developing Change Teams

An effective focus on leadership development, including adaptive change principles and ethical decision-making, will help train people throughout your workforce to be prepared to be part of any change initiative. Building an effective coalition for change is about empowering individuals and recognizing the need for representation across multiple internal constituencies. Any call for system change that doesn't involve the applicable parts of that system will fail, both in cultural and practical adoption.

The difficulty is in mapping out which parts of the system matter for which change initiatives. I've already mentioned that it's not effective to have the entire organization involved in, or aware of, every single change effort, and that every effort cannot effectively be blessed by the CEO. What that means is we need a road map for how to build a coalition for the particular change initiative—not the last one, not the one that's going to come next, but the one that's right in front of us.

When developing change teams for organizations, I not only ask that the teams reflect multiple constituencies across the organization, but I also often look across the org chart for representation from multiple parts of the hierarchy. I'm especially wary of change teams composed of senior executives. Oftentimes a title that is too high on the org chart sucks all the oxygen out of a room that would otherwise be creative about its approach to problem-solving.

Nothing kills innovation faster than all heads in the room turning to see what a CEO thinks. This approach also helps develop young leaders. Employees who are hungry for change are often also hungry for new opportunities to learn, and being a part of an internal coalition gives them an opportunity to flex their leadership skills and add feathers to their professional development caps.

That isn't to say that senior leadership buy-in to a change initiative isn't important—the opposite! Senior leadership that isn't completely aware of or bought into what is happening on the ground with a change initiative can completely kill the momentum for change. All it takes is one C-suite leader to veto a great idea from the change team, and suddenly a coalition that was functioning with representatives across the organization has people backing into their respective corners again. The snowflake model worked for campaigns because it not only distributed responsibility, but the model itself also created an infrastructure for sending information and feedback back up the chain of command to headquarters.

Senior leadership has to be kept aware of the change team's direction to the best of its ability. When working with internal coalitions, we'll often strategize about internal communications specifically as a separate work stream to make sure enough consideration is being given to how internal stakeholders are being brought along.

I've mapped out one way to think about criteria for developing an internal change team in the two-by-two on the figure on page 152, where the x-axis is representation from applicable departments affected by a specific change need, and the y-axis represents decision makers from across the org chart, with considerations and challenges for each quadrant. To be clear, I've seen change initiatives work with team makeups that look like all four, but the teams that look like the upper-right quadrant always have a better chance of success.

Mapping Change Team Participants

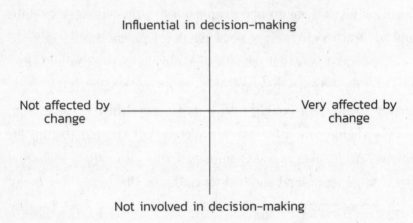

Influential in decision-making

Not affected by change | Very affected by change

Not involved in decision-making

Ultimately, effective change teams are going to have a few things in common:

- **Shared purpose:** When people are brought together who don't normally work with one another, it's important to establish a vision, ideally as a subset to a clear organizational mission, for what the team is trying to accomplish. Coalitions working on complicated system changes need to need each other. If one person or department dominates the output, parts of the coalition will become disillusioned and will eventually disengage.
- **Clear norms:** One exercise we often have new change teams do up front is to set their expectations on the table. How do the team members expect to communicate? How often will they meet? Who'll be responsible for which work streams,

and how will the rest of the team be kept up to date with progress? Being explicit up front helps stymie headaches and hurt feelings later.

- **Diverse skill sets:** Do we have both dimensions of leadership represented—natural managers and natural emotional leaders? Is the expertise represented appropriate for the kind of change we're undertaking? For example, if technology adoption is a major goal, do we have people on the team who understand that technology inside and out?

One big consideration when forming a team is whether to intentionally include detractors, people who are doubtful about the need for the change initiative or skeptical of its success. I've sometimes counseled clients to include detractors as a way of forcing them to get skin in the game. Once they have their fingerprints on a direction, they are often more inclined to merchandise it to others and are often powerful advocates because of their story of initial skepticism. Whether or not to include them on the team has to do with their motivations. Are they skeptical because of failed change initiatives in the past or because they can't see a path forward on implementation? Being a part of the team may help overcome those doubts and may help others on the team see risks to implementation that enthusiasts would have overlooked. But if they are dissenting only from a place of cynicism, or if their doubts come from a place of bitterness or sense that the organization has harmed them personally, their sour grapes may become too much for a team that needs to be comfortable operating with a relative amount of ambiguity and trust.

As representatives of a change coalition, teams ultimately need to model the flexibility and adaptive thinking that should be an emergent property of the entire coalition, qualities that are not inherent in any organization used to doing things a certain way. Change team leaders have to become the first line of defense against a status quo mentality, and they need the backing of those in power to be able to do so. Leadership is about modeling just as much as it is about saying the right things, and change team leaders have to model becoming comfortable with—even excited about—the unknown.

Coalitions of the Wheeling

Have you ever stopped to watch a kettle of birds? A kettle happens when the birds wheel and circle about in the air, readying themselves for a big migration. Call it a form of bird-to-bird communication. The wheeling serves as a way to gain altitude and strength, as well as signal an announcement and a call to action: *Hey! We're going somewhere. Are you ready?*

During my undergrad days at Baylor, I used to watch thousands, and I mean *thousands,* of common grackles fly around campus. It used to feel like a Hitchcock moment was imminent. The strange and wonderful sight of them wheeling in the air, preparing to keep moving on their annual fall migration, stuck with me as a metaphor right when I began to study the history of people movements, theology, and business. Because the truth is that all significant movements, whether big or small, have to change direction at some point. Changing direction can be a life-and-death moment for a coalition.

As circumstances change, so does a change in the political or ethical calculus about a strategy. We've already covered how hard it is for us to change our minds once committed to an idea; now imagine trying to seed a change when a crowd of people is committed to moving in one direction, especially one in which they already have an emotional commitment. Leadership when a change in direction is warranted becomes not just about organizing people, but also about reorganizing them without burning them out. George Carlin said that "inside every cynical person, there is a disappointed idealist." So how do we adjust expectations without disappointing our supporters?

Senator Bernie Sanders may be one of the best movement builders of the past decade. After having run two unsuccessful bids for the presidency, the senator created a following of progressive idealists dedicated to moving the Democratic Party to the left. Senator Sanders is largely seen as being credible on progressive issues because of his uncompromising dedication to his ideals. It's a wonder, then, that he became so pragmatic about getting things done during the Biden presidency, especially on infrastructure. His commitment to spend on progressive priorities didn't stop him from being a passionate advocate for bills that may not have had everything he wanted in them. His supporters were listening, too. One of the pro-Sanders advocacy groups, Our Revolution, rebranded itself as pragmatically progressive in July 2021. Leadership has a role to play not only in signaling a change in direction, but also in getting others in influential positions to follow that change and to communicate clearly to the constituencies they represent.

In 2018 and 2019, 18 Coffees, backed by a group of foundations, ran a series of experiments with a coalition of community organizations dedicated to immigration and American citizenship. We wanted to know what kinds of digital strategies and tactics could support the on-the-ground work being done by nonprofits to help green card holders applying for citizenship. Over two years we created several hypotheses with different digital components, all supported with expertise and engagement by the groups on the ground. Just like any good experiment, the data helped us pivot several times—and the on-the-ground organizations had to pivot with us. The leadership of those organizations and the staff doing the work were critical to our learning process. Over time, we were able to add thousands of people into the queue to become citizens.

Leading a change coalition only works if that coalition has the flexibility to adapt. Stressing up front that change will be an adaptive process helps set expectations for change teams, executive leadership, and the entire organization, and gets everyone involved in the learning process.

Avoiding Death by Committee

For some reason, no matter the problem, almost every organization I've worked with has felt the need to start by throwing a committee or task force at it. I've encountered committees dedicated to diversity, equity, and inclusion; digital transformation; and other big, intractable problems that no group of people talking at each other has a chance in hell of solving. Committees are the easy way out. They have all the feel-good qualities of a coalition with none of the teeth to actually get anything done.

The difference between a committee and a change team is one of outputs and expectations. Committees inevitably have low credibility within an organization because their output is ultimately only probative. They make recommendations that senior executives get to follow or not follow. And let's be honest. The executives themselves often add color to the recommendations before they are finalized, tainting any hope of being objective. Committees are ultimately an act of political cowardice, a way to give the organization a feeling of forward momentum without making any hard decisions that may offend one constituency or another. They are a desperate act by paralyzed leadership.

If it seems like I'm being too harsh on committees, please find my contact information in the back of this book and send me one example of a committee you've seen work like it was intended to. I'd genuinely like to hear about it because I've seen exactly zero in my career with any real influence.

Change teams, by contrast, represent the different constituencies of the organization but are actually empowered to act on their own instincts. Senior leadership is kept in the loop with their progress, but the teams have operational authority to make change where they see fit. Ideally, they also have time dedicated to the change initiative, as we'll talk about in the next chapter, baked into their roles and job performance metrics, whereas people on committees are usually giving their time above and beyond their day-to-day responsibilities. Change teams have the awesome responsibility to imagine the change, implement the change, and merchandise the change. Committees are lucky if they get to do the imagining part well.

Every committee or task force I've seen runs into inevitable political inertia. Once management realizes that the task force has no chance of success, the group enters a death spiral of irrelevance, as membership participation dwindles and recommendations fail to grab the attention of the organization. In addition to lacking the authority to make any change, committees lack the shared sense of purpose that can come from being in the trenches with people doing the work, making it even easier for each department to look out for its own interests instead of those of the organization or its mission.

Mobilizing change teams out of relevant constituencies within the organization is approaching the work of transformation with an organizer's mindset and is a much more effective way of tackling adaptive change. In a no-point-B environment, committees slow an organization down when it should be speeding up.

Changing a complex organization is hard work, and it takes a great deal of effort over time by many people. An effective coalition for change can not only help scale the transformation effort and make it move faster, but it can also add an energy around the change that is infectious. When people feel like they have ownership over the direction of their job, they get excited about participating. And when they feel like the direction of their job will make the world, not just the company, better, they become dedicated to the entire mission's success.

7

How to Work in Public

On October 1, 2013, the new health care marketplaces opened, and the president's legacy was on the line. One of the most important parts of the implementation of the Affordable Care Act, a signature accomplishment of the Obama presidency, was the launch of the federally managed Healthcare.gov and corresponding state marketplaces. This was meant to be a new era in coverage for millions of Americans—especially those who had been previously denied because of preexisting conditions—unable to get affordable insurance through their employers. A mentor of mine had framed it up to us like so: if Healthcare.gov fails, a generation of people will lose faith in the government to solve problems.

The launch didn't go smoothly. The technology behind Health-care.gov had been besieged with problems and rushed to market anyway. If it had been any other product, the launch date would have been pushed back, but the website had to launch on October 1 no matter what due to provisions in the law. For weeks, users trying to enroll ran into issues. Stories in the press were relentless, with headlines like "Health Site Woes Undermine Obama's Vow on Government" in the *New York Times*. By the time the marketplace was up and running smoothly in early December, more than two months of the six-month open enrollment period had passed with depressingly few people enrolled. The Department of Health and Human Services had estimated that six million people would sign up, a public milestone that had been set as a benchmark for marketplace health. We were already very behind.

Once we were given the green light to direct people to sign up, our team threw everything we had at getting people enrolled. We worked with partners on coordinated campaigns in the media. We launched television, out-of-home, and a barrage of digital advertisements. Our digital team tracked people through enrollment to follow up with those whom we suspected hadn't completed their sign-up process. And our creative team came up with dozens of campaigns focused on catching the attention especially of those whom we called the young invincibles, healthy young adults who were typically not conscious of their health insurance needs and whom the marketplace needed to balance out the flood of those joining with high health care costs.

In one of those campaigns, a young staff member on my team, Ethan, did a photo shoot as a young invincible returning home to his family for the holidays. The campaign was aimed at parents, persuading them to talk to their adult children about getting health insurance while their kids were home visiting. It also had a tongue-in-cheek tone, as Ethan pretended to enjoy all the comforts of home again as a young adult who gets to enjoy being a kid again, including having hot chocolate in his pajamas.

Over the last few weeks in December, we ran hundreds of pieces of content featuring Ethan across ad campaigns, email, and social media, but one particular creative piece in a tweet caught the attention of right-wing media pundits, who began criticizing it for what they saw as the feminization of American men. The image caught fire: what started as an army of Twitter trolls quickly gained traction across the rest of the internet and eventually made its way onto Fox News. For two days #PajamaBoy trended. People began photoshopping Ethan into images with Obama, Rachel Maddow, and other figures of the left; they dug up his parents' address and essays he had written in college. For a few days in 2013, Ethan was the focus of the American right's antipathy.

Throughout the manufactured scandal, Ethan acted like a champ. He had done improv and other acting in Chicago and had developed a thick skin about criticism. But we knew that kind of attention would get to anyone. Our digital team wanted to show our support for him. So two days into the event, Ethan walked into the office only to find every one of his teammates dressed in pajamas as a show of solidarity.

Over the next few months, we refocused on the end goal of getting people covered and ran several more campaigns in concert with our partners and volunteers. At the end of the open enrollment period in March 2014, 7.1 million people had signed up on the health care marketplaces. Ethan was the one who hit send on the tweet announcing the final numbers.

I've learned a lot about workplaces that work over my career, but the experience of being in a high-stakes environment with people earnestly trying to do the right thing—sometimes at great personal expense—taught me the most about what it means to have a mission-driven workplace that is capable of adaptation. We need more work environments that inspire commitment and creativity from employees, or else we won't be capable of the kind of transformative effort the new conscious economy is demanding.

Employee Experience in an Adaptive World

In February 2020, 18 Coffees had been a fully distributed workforce for a few years, but my business partner and I decided to get a private office space for our Chicago-based employees as a home base—right before the world shut down due to the coronavirus pandemic. Obviously, we were taken off guard because of our new commitment to the lease, but because of our distributed work culture, it was easy for us to shift back into remote work. Most of our clients were not so lucky.

We had been talking to our clients about the future of work for years, but now we were presented with a once-in-a-generation opportunity to completely reimagine how our clients' business was done. Many came to us asking about the technical details of remote work (e.g., some had no laptops for their employees and no remote information security protocols), but the most imaginative came asking about new growth opportunities, employee engagement, and other creative ways to turn the crisis into an opportunity. To paraphrase the economist Paul Romer, they realized a crisis is a terrible thing to waste.

The business response to the pandemic showed that despite all our talk about the future of work, most companies had structured work the same way for decades, never really letting go of the management-centric thinking that had dominated business for the past one hundred years. Executives talked a big talk about technology in the workplace, power shifting to employees, and other trends that mimicked what was happening in the public sphere, but most had never made any real moves to give up their power or mobilize their employees. Within the walls of major corporations, the status quo can be a powerful force.

It's important to acknowledge that the future of work is here right now because (as previously argued) our constant focus on what's coming has created present risk and some very real workplace inadequacies. While we obsess over the role of hybrid work and what the next office will look like, our employees of color are still dissatisfied with our efforts toward creating a more equitable environment. While we look to new cloud-based personal productivity tools, employee engagement is at an all-time low, with only 36 percent of employees feeling truly engaged in their work in the first half of 2021, according to the polling firm Gallup. Just like any other change initiative, we need workplaces that are constantly changing to meet the burden of the Angelouian principle of knowing better and then doing better.

Recent research has shown how unimpressed employees are by perks employers have offered throughout the past decade. Having a Ping-Pong table at your office always had the potential to be window dressing for a toxic corporate culture, but many people spent over a year during the pandemic not going into an office at all. Strip away the shiny objects, and what is left?

Now that we're in a tighter labor market, more workers are calling BS on perks that don't matter as employers try to compete for talent. So what really matters to the new workforce? I believe it's the same perks that have always mattered, but now that everything else has been stripped away, we can see them for what they are: a focus on outcomes, not hours; the right to self-determination; and a mission that matters.

Even before the pandemic, forward-thinking organizations were redefining how they measured employee success, focusing on work results, not work appearance. Instead of a butts-in-seats mentality that focused on the amount of time employees spent at the office, they offered outcomes as the ultimate indicator of success. Combined with a project and deliverables focus that helps teams home in on outputs, a results-driven work environment can be a powerful motivator.

For example, we have a nonprofit client at 18 Coffees that saw the pandemic-required switch to remote work as a rare opportunity to completely reimagine how it measured worker productivity. Instead of worrying about visibility into each other's work, they slashed meeting schedules in half and incentivized a focus on program outcomes in order to rally their workforce during a hard time for their community. The results? An increase in productivity impressed their donors enough to blow past their typical annual fundraising goal.

Related to an ability to focus on the work instead of work performance is the idea that your work has to be done at any specific time in any specific way. One silver lining of the pandemic was that the artificial boundaries between our work and personal lives came down as we managed childcare, pets, and all sorts of distractions while on a flurry of video conferencing calls with our coworkers.

Let's not go back. Pay your workers the respect of giving them clear guidelines, then allow them to do the work as they see fit, where they see fit. Mutual trust is the only way hybrid work will work. Too many companies have embraced remote work only to spy on how employees spend their time, or have embraced a hybrid approach to being in the office only to dictate exactly what days employees need to have their butts in their seats.

I once had a mentor say of the culture I was hired into, "We're not a third-grade classroom. We don't require you to be in your seat at a specific time with your uniform on. Just be an adult, and get your work done." I had just had my second child. At the time, it was the best perk I could have asked for.

There's never been a better time to redefine why your organization exists with an eye toward attracting talent that increasingly cares about purpose at work. But I actually think how we talk about purpose is too often individualized and divorced from larger conversations about what the company stands for and how it exists in our social environment—something about which employees are increasingly concerned.

A better approach is to talk about mission—how the company's purpose gets activated in the world—and what role each person has in that mission. Being a part of a team doing something meaningful is an incredible motivator. If Drucker was right about knowledge workers being treated like volunteers, then what motivates volunteers should motivate workers—and volunteers give their time for something they believe in.

When I worked in politics, we worked through all kinds of uncomfortable conditions (sparse, ugly, and uncomfortable offices are hallmarks of political campaigns) because the end goal mattered more than our circumstances. The perk of doing something that matters in the trenches with a team you love trumps all kinds of workplace luxuries and can help motivate employees when things get hard.

Why do I think these three cultural fundamentals are still perks that attract workers to a company? Because so few work environments still reflect any of them. Now that we've realized work isn't a place, we have an opportunity to change our cultures to focus on what really matters to the people who enter our doors every day (physically or otherwise), instead of covering up toxic workplace issues with shiny objects. Real workplace benefits are innate to the culture, and culture is an output of purpose and practice.

Rather than focus on all the ways the workplace still needs to improve, rather than addressing a specific topic like inclusion in the workplace—which, let's be honest, other people have already written amazing books about—let's talk about what our workplace needs to look like in order to move at the new speed of change. If we're going to create an organization nimble enough to address some of those topics, we need to continue to focus on making the organization we have now capable of both adaptive and technical change.

Workplace Teams Versus Families

In August 2020, Tobi Lütke, CEO of the e-commerce platform Shopify, sent a letter to his managers outlining what he saw as the company's drift from its core mission into distracting social issues. The letter received much attention for its core idea: we are not a family:

> Shopify, like any other for-profit company, is not a family. The very idea is preposterous. You are born into a family. You never choose it, and they can't un-family you. It should be massively obvious that Shopify is not a family but I see people, even leaders, casually use terms like "shopifam" which will cause the members of our teams (especially junior ones that have never worked anywhere else) to get the wrong impression. The dangers of "family thinking" are that it becomes incredibly hard to let poor performers go. Shopify is a team, not a family.
>
> We literally only want the best people in the world. The reason why you joined Shopify is because—I hope—all the other people you met during the interview process were really smart, caring, and committed. This is magic and it creates a virtuous magnetism on talented people because very few people in the world have this in themselves. People who don't should not be part of this team. This magic and magnetism is a product of tight performance management that I expect all of us to get back to.
>
> Shopify is also not the government. We cannot solve every societal problem here. We are part of an ecosystem, of economies, of culture, and of actual countries. We also can't take care of all your needs. We will try our best to take care of the ones that ensure you can support our mission.

Shopify's worldview is well documented—we believe in liberal values and equality of opportunity. Sometimes we see opportunities to help nudge these causes forward. We do this because this directly helps our business and our merchants and not because of some moralistic overreach.

On its surface, I believe the argument about being a team versus a family is a healthy one. Too many leaders over the past few decades, in their pursuit of commitment to the work, have pushed the family narrative in the workplace without concern for how that narrative tends to push workers into violating their own work-life boundaries. Often, "we're like a family here" is code for "we want to be your priority before anything else."

I also believe like Lütke that the family narrative, though it sounds warm and fuzzy, actually makes it harder for a company to fulfill its mission, even if that mission has warm and fuzzy social impact implications. We're stuck with family members no matter what, even if we disagree with their values or their performance. High-performing teams on a mission to make the world better can't afford dead weight. The Obama team was incredibly close, but the stakes were so high that we couldn't afford to carry anyone who wasn't committed.

Where Lütke's analysis gets tricky is in his assertion that Shopify is "not the government." It is true that businesses should not believe they can solve complex social issues that are the responsibility of the public sector. (In fact, one of President Obama's critiques of business leaders who used to tell him that government needed to function more like a business was to explain to them that unlike the private sector, government couldn't pick and choose which constituents were its target audience. Every person mattered.) In *Winners Take All*, published in 2019, Anand Giridharadas offered a biting critique of wealthy business leaders thinking they know better than the public sector about public policy, claiming we'd all be better off if we just taxed the wealthy and spent more as a public body on social programs. But what I think Giridharadas's and Lütke's analyses miss is employee and customer expectations for business leaders to participate in making the world better. In the 2021 Edelman Trust Barometer, business was listed as the highest trusted institution: 61 percent of people surveyed trusted business over NGOs (57 percent), government (53 percent) and media (51 percent). "The high expectations of business to address and solve today's challenges has never been more apparent," the report claimed.

Shopify had already been forced to participate in public discussions in a myriad of ways, including taking down sites affiliated with President Trump after the January 6 raid on the Capitol, and committing publicly to donations to the NAACP Legal Defense Fund and Campaign Zero after the killing of George Floyd. They'd also been criticized for their longtime hosting of the online store of Breitbart, the right-wing news organization that regularly publishes inflammatory and offensive content. Lütke's assertion that the company engaging on issues that didn't directly affect their merchants was "moralistic overreach" betrayed how the company had a track record of doing so already. Whether they were forced to by outside or inside pressure, their employees were watching. According to some employees at the time, Lütke's open letter, no matter the merits of its argument, felt like an opportunistic way to silence debate. Why could the company speak up externally about its values, but its employees couldn't debate internally?

Lütke isn't the only CEO in recent years struggling with the role of their businesses as it relates to social issues. The CEOs of Delta and Coca-Cola were dragged into political issues in their home state of Georgia after the Republican legislature there passed restrictions on voting. The CEO of Coinbase was criticized (and in some circles, celebrated) for his declaration in late 2020 that Coinbase would be a "politically neutral" workplace that would explicitly discourage the championing of social issues. As a business leader in a complex world, with employees increasingly expecting to bring their values to work, how should today's leaders approach building a workplace culture that can adapt as social expectations change?

Alternatives to Hierarchy

In a work environment where employees have broad leeway to determine their own way to achieve project-based outcomes, always with an eye toward achieving a larger mission, the need to micromanage employee outcomes becomes less important. Employees are more satisfied with project-based workplaces, and work environments that are more focused on project outcomes than work outputs are more capable of solving adaptive problems. They also require less hierarchy in order to move quickly.

Don't get me wrong. I don't advocate for a completely hierarchy-less organization. I believe the binary choice of either hierarchy or distributed decision-making is a false one. In reality, most organizations need empowered teams with a certain amount of self-determination tackling adaptive problems across the organization, and a sense of responsibility for success at multiple layers of the organization. Even the most grassroots of organizing movements has failed without clear leadership.

In many ways, the conversation about the benefits and pitfalls of hierarchy mimics the false binary choice about freedom versus control within an organization. When a company has an internal debate about where to give its employees freedoms versus paint-by-numbers structure, the paint-by-numbers will always win. Employees will default to what feels safest, and managers will default to evaluating what they most understand. Freedom is messy, but it has also been clearly tied, in study after study, to better job performance.

The eyeglasses retailer Warby Parker took the concept of freedom and democratizing the workplace to the extreme when it created an internal employee decision-making process called Warbles. Company leaders wanted a new way to increase productivity, and they found it by launching a company marketplace for employee ideas. The process allows any employee to nominate programming projects they think would benefit the company's mission, and for others to vote on their favorite ideas, incentivizing people to organize their peers around their ideas. The programmers have autonomy to choose which projects to focus on but are rewarded for choosing ones with the most votes. Similarly, teams compete to accumulate the most points, with a reward given every quarter. By decreasing management oversight of team priorities, Warby Parker found a way to increase team excitement and productivity without increasing overhead.

Warby Parker is also famously a mission-driven employer, one of the first to pioneer a buy-one-give-one model for its direct-to-consumer glasses. As the company has scaled, it has kept mission at its core. Amazing things happen when employees have a clear understanding of a company's mission and clear guidelines to help them understand their role in it, and then are set loose to take action. True mission-driven work is inspiring and keeps people moving forward through ambiguity and even frustration. I've seen time and again, just like Ethan overcoming the pajama incident, how resilient empowered, mission-driven employees can be.

Modern employees need to be taught not only operational guidelines, but ethical ones as well. Frameworks have to be put in place to guide ethical decision-making that is grounded in clear boundaries the company has delineated for itself. Too often I've seen company leaders leave the guiding of ethical norms to a few HR-driven trainings that are more about compliance than ethical behavior—or, worse, expect doing the right thing to be self-explanatory. The world is too complex to leave the right thing to chance. As we'll discuss in the final chapter, employees need a strong north star for when hard decisions have to be made, and clear operating principles for how to execute on that bigger vision. But that doesn't mean every employee decision has to be micromanaged to ensure ethical behavior. How would that even work? Companies need strong ethical guidelines, but ultimately, they need a strong culture of trust. You have to hire the right people, train them, and then trust them to make the right decisions.

We've already discussed how the pursuit of power is a corrupting influence on many leaders. Competition is a hell of a drug. But many have a hard time abdicating decision-making power because they did such a great job navigating the bureaucracy to get where they are, and they perceive those decisions to be very important.

I empathize with those instincts as a business owner. It's hard not to want to be involved in every major initiative my company undertakes. But my involvement doesn't help 18 Coffees scale, and it can be demoralizing for my people. Sometimes the best thing we can do to help our companies innovate is to step out of the way and let an adaptive organization go to work.

Adaptive Organizations

Most organizational change initiatives focus on the project management essentials, often with the end goal of implementing some new process, technology, or team. This is a necessary part of changing and is often the easiest part to wrap one's head around because it has a clear end point. This is called technical change, and it's the part of change management that has an actual point B. But stopping there is a mistake.

When we only focus on the technical change, we completely miss the necessity of enabling our organizational culture to change with the technical change. The best new technology is going to fail without the business process around it changing. If a sales team upgrades its CRM platform to provide new opportunities for client visibility and cross-network collaboration but fails to actually change the behavior of its sales reps to use the new CRM versus their more comfortable spreadsheets, the implementation may have worked from a purely technical standpoint, but the organization didn't adapt. Adaptive change is the cornerstone of modern change management because it marries process and culture.

But adaptive change is much harder for a team to wrap its head around than technical change. Adaptive change has no point B; it is a practice, a discipline. And just like anything else that takes practice, it easily gets rusty. Organizations need to master both kinds of change, but I've likened adaptive change to exercise. If you don't get the reps in, your muscles will atrophy. If you don't run the miles, you'll lose your cardio fitness. Teams get comfortable, people turn over, and before you know it, the culture stagnates and doesn't adapt as quickly.

Top-down organizations with cultures defined by hierarchy have a hard time with adaptive change. It makes sense when you think about how these organizations have traditionally gone about the practice of strategy. Classic management thinking meant strategy was decided at the top, the strategy dictated the structure needed to execute it, and that structure required systems to execute key business functions. People became cogs in the larger corporate machine, and changing that machine meant a top-down effort to shift strategy, which was often like trying to steer the Titanic away from an iceberg. Every problem became a technical problem and some shift in structure was needed to operate differently.

Resourceful organizations think about strategy with the lens of adaptive change. Instead of taking a strategy-structure-systems approach, they look at organizational effectiveness through the lens of mission, priorities, and workstreams. The mission gives shape to the strategy, which dictates priorities, not structures, and from those priorities flow workstreams and deliverables. Employees have broad leeway to engage in those workstreams the best way they see fit in order to achieve the mission.

Smart organizations do three things to practice adaptive change: they train leaders in adaptive change practices; they dedicate specific resources to the demand for constant change; and they distribute ownership of change throughout the organization.

We covered in the last chapter how important it is to build new change leaders as a part of creating coalitions for change that represent all your internal constituencies, and how storytelling is one of the most effective tools in a leaders' toolkit. But leaders mastered in adaptive change need more than just good communication and organizing skills; they need to be able to diagnose and respond to disruptive issues quickly so that any coalition they build will have a clear problem to solve. Change leaders need the instincts of adaptive change, which comes through intentional training and practice.

Organizations that take the need for adaptive change seriously don't think about change only when some specific technical change effort presents itself. They dedicate resources (time, talent, budget) to adaptive challenges proactively. At 18 Coffees, we've worked with several clients to develop long-standing change teams that tackle different technical challenges as they arise. The teams focus on building an adaptive culture that can tackle any change initiative, encouraging the kind of organizational citizenship behavior that leads to the identification of problems and opportunities outside of people's formal job descriptions. This kind of forward-thinking investment takes guts because it's often seen as an opportunity cost for people's time on the team that could be used on something else in the short term. But those who have the capability to tackle fast-moving problems never regret the investment when such a problem presents itself, as it inevitably does.

Distributing ownership throughout an organization means that anyone should feel empowered to see a need, call for change, and feel like they will be heard. Conversations about new opportunities and threats in the marketplace should be able to travel up and down the org chart with equal ease while teams are given flexibility to tackle adaptive problems as they arise. Because frontline workers have the most exposure to the work, they are the ones who see a need first and can implement solutions more quickly. But frontline workers will never do that if they feel like their concerns won't be heard. To truly create a sense of ownership, organizations have to be structured in a way that doesn't feel oppressive or overly controlled. If a call for change has a long journey up an org chart through several different power structures, it's going to lose momentum. Hierarchy should support the culture without oppressing it.

Moral Entrepreneurship

I've always been fascinated by Plato's concept of a philosopher-king, someone who is not only an effective ruler, but who is also truly curious and loves knowledge for the sake of knowledge. Ethical leaders in the new economy, one in which what we think we know is constantly changing, have to be similarly curious if they want to be effective at leading their organizations toward something better than they are today. Anyone looking to be a chief executive now has to operate with a certain amount of moral imagination (and fewer authoritarian instincts than in Plato's time).

Leaders no longer have the luxury of myopically focusing on their own business goals. The world was always more interconnected than that. But now your employees have visibility into how much your business decisions have cascading effects on society—and believe me, they care about those effects. True leadership is about empowering your people to make the kind of change they want to see within your organization so that they can feel good about the kind of impact your organization has on the world. And you don't need to trade business success to do it! On the contrary, I've seen many organizations move in a more ethical direction without compromising their performance metrics. It just takes a more holistic view of what success means for your company.

When coffee giant Starbucks was faced with a controversy over the arrests of two Black men in a Philadelphia location in April of 2018, CEO Kevin Johnson moved swiftly to denounce the arrest and eventually, in consultation with experts from the Equal Justice Initiative, Demos, and the NAACP Legal Defense and Educational Fund, announced a one-day mandatory racial bias training for all of its 175,000 US-based employees. It was a bold move designed to make a statement about Starbucks' commitment to its inclusive values, but it was also costly. Bloomberg estimated at the time that the cost of the one-day shutdown would be more than $16 million. Investors were nervous, but Johnson positioned the bold response as paying "long-term dividends for Starbucks."

Milton Friedman's position that the "social responsibility of a business is to increase its profits" is a simplistic mantra that corporate leaders have used to spare themselves the responsibility of engaging on public issues for decades. But Johnson and other leaders are beginning to look at a longer timeline, where social responsibility and fiduciary responsibility start to merge.

The rise of ESG metrics shows that investors are also beginning to be willing to think beyond short-term quarterly profits to the long-term impact of a company's social and environmental practices. The truth is that shareholder primacy was always an incredibly myopic perspective for a complex world, but it provided a simplified version of leadership ethics that acted as a comfort blanket for CEOs who didn't want to think about anything beyond their company's walls. Moral leadership can no longer be outsourced.

There is growing evidence that employees will reward what they perceive to be ethical leadership. A 2011 study by the *International Journal of Hospitality Management* demonstrated a positive correlation between ethical leadership by executives and hotel managers' job satisfaction and organizational commitment. In 2014, the *Journal of Business Ethics* published a study showing that not only does ethical leadership by supervisors have a positive effect on individual contributors' job performance, but it is also more likely to tie an individual's goals with those of the organization. And the 2021 Edelman Trust Barometer found that belief-driven employees are more likely to stay with the company for years and recommend the company to others.

Increasingly, competitive advantage will be earned by leaders who not only demonstrate normative ethical leadership—as defined by appropriate moral conduct and encouragement of followers to do the same—but who also push the boundaries of ethical norms through demonstrated social engagement.

In 2015, Dan Price, CEO of credit card processing company Gravity Payments, found out one of his employees was working a second job at a local McDonald's in order to make ends meet. Convinced that no one at his company should have to work two jobs, he announced he would cut his own $1 million salary by 90 percent in order to raise his employees' salaries to a minimum of $70,000 a year—a benchmark for happiness and well-being from a 2010 study by Princeton University professors Angus Deaton and Daniel Kahneman. He received immediate harsh criticism from a cadre of trickle-down business pundits. But six years later he was able to announce a three-fold revenue increase, as his employees bought homes, had children, paid down debt, and maintained a fierce loyalty to the company through the downturn of the pandemic. Price's bold decision shifted the Overton window for employee pay.

Most business leaders are responding to moral issues as they arise in news cycles, dragging their organizations along as the concept of what is considered ethical business behavior shifts out from under them. This kind of reactive posture is understandable when the stakes for missteps are so high. But the future belongs to the moral entrepreneurs, those willing to push their organization beyond a reactive moral posture in order to realize a new kind of business environment, better than anyone has so far imagined.

8

Fly with Both Eyes Open

I studied philosophy as an undergrad, even functioning as a teaching assistant at one point for a course that covered thinkers from Plato to Rousseau. But one of the best philosophical lessons I learned about life came from a season of the NBC series *The Good Place*. (Spoilers ahead for those who haven't watched.)

The main characters have discovered that a points system determines someone's fate in the afterlife, but that point system is flawed. No one has made it to the Good Place (the show's version of heaven) in centuries. Michael, the show's demon antihero, determines it's because the complexity of modern life leads to unintended negative moral consequences for every decision. Humans can't earn their way into the Good Place because every good thing they do turns out bad.

Michael makes an appeal to Judge Gen, the all-knowing judge of the universe, that humans can't possibly understand the consequences of their decisions: "These days, just buying a tomato at the grocery store means you are unwittingly supporting toxic pesticides, exploited labor, contributing to global warming. Humans think they're making one choice, but they're actually making dozens of choices they don't even know they're making." The judge decides to see for herself, and after spending a comically short amount of time on Earth, agrees with Michael that humans may be better than their point totals suggest.

What I loved about the show was how beautifully it illustrated the complexity of modern decision-making. In the last few hundred years, as the world has become increasingly interconnected with global economies and global supply chains—not to mention connected with digital information at a moment's notice—each decision we make as consumers reverberates more than we could ever imagine. And each decision as business leaders we place in front of consumers has the opportunity to do good or create harm for them and for our business.

In today's economy, business leaders have to master complexity thinking in order not to create moral hazard for their employees, customers, and other stakeholders. But we can do more than that. Understanding complexity points us away from business decisions to avoid and toward positive changes we can make in the way we do business in order to minimize moral hazard as well as maximize moral entrepreneurship. Complexity can be paralyzing, but we don't have to let it keep us from thinking creatively about the way we do business.

In order to navigate complexity, it helps to understand the many ways complexity presents itself in our business decisions. Complexity arises out of system dynamics inherent to running a business in the modern world. It is informed by ambiguity, uncertainty, and emergent data that complicates our ability to make clear decisions. And, finally, complexity arises out of the mess we are as humans. As individuals and as groups, we are complex systems ourselves.

I won't spoil the conclusion of *The Good Place*. Suffice it to say that the points system does eventually get reconsidered. Humans are given second chances, and complexity is acknowledged as a tough part of moving through the modern world. Operating with perfect moral clarity was an idea ripe for satire.

Understanding Complex Ecosystems

Two years ago, my son's school was doing a science experiment involving plants as a way to understand biological ecosystems. They'd learned about the importance of rainforests, how trees provide life for the entire planet. And now they were growing plants in their classroom, and we were tasked with planting seeds and helping nurture a plant to grow at home.

My five-year-old son had a hard time wrapping his head around how from one little seed an entire forest could grow. I had to explain that one little seed made a tree, which made thousands more seeds, which made millions more trees. I'm pretty sure I was in the middle of explaining exponential growth when he got bored and left to play with his Lego set. But that conversation stuck in my mind, as I had parallel conversations with business leaders in the years after.

Think about what an absurd concept an enterprise actually is. Companies exist as ecosystems, within the ecosystem of society, made up of individual ecosystems that we call humans. If complexity increases as the number of component parts added to a system increases, enterprises are highly complex systems surrounded by and made up of highly complex systems. The thought of trying to manage complexity from that point of view is enough to make one's head spin.

As a small company, my business partner and I handle most of our operations and logistics (she handles much more than I do). And we often work with larger enterprises on complex organizational challenges, which means we are often working with larger enterprise procurement and legal teams to stand up our projects and receive our payments.

One such operation for a larger client just about ground our small company to a halt. After negotiating the terms of the project with our main client contacts, we were sent to their procurement team to finalize the payment terms, then to their legal team to negotiate the contract details, and then to their third-party payment system to set up payment details, all over the course of several weeks. This kind of process is not uncommon, but each department's operations in this particular company were exceptionally disconnected from the others. Someone from the procurement team would tell us one thing, then someone from legal would tell us another. The payment vendor couldn't manage terms that we'd agreed to separately with the other teams. Each arm of the company was operating in such a silo that they were unaware of how the machine was grinding up our small company and spitting us out.

Seeing a large enterprise as not just an organic system but a machine with its own desires that moves in a specific direction despite the individual desires of its parts helps us understand why complexity theorist Edgar Morin has claimed "to limit oneself to a heteroproductive vision of the enterprise would be insufficient, because by producing things and services the enterprise also produces itself." Enterprises maintain themselves through the act of production, and in this case, our client's machine was producing our engagement as its outcome. From our perspective, it was a complicated, inefficient process. From the enterprise's perspective, everything was happening as it should. Each component part of the enterprise was producing its part in the production process.

Managing complexity is not about control but about balance. Morin has said, "The only way to fight against degeneration is permanent regeneration." Markets are self-organized out of chaos, at once both organized and completely random. And as much as we like to believe otherwise, so are our companies. Too much order and there would be no innovation or creativity; too much disorder and we are paralyzed by unpredictability. Every organization, like every other living ecosystem, needs to degenerate to some degree in order to regenerate. Cleansing forest fires provide fodder for new life to grow, even as they painfully burn down the old version of life.

Coming out of a global pandemic, our society finds itself in a poignant moment of overt disorder that is affecting the enterprise ecosystems that operate within it. Organizations that prove themselves capable of regeneration, capable of doing the hard work of change in this moment, are the ones that will survive long into the future.

Uncertainty and Emergence

Let's tackle the hard stuff first. Uncertainty is one of the hallmarks of complexity theory, and one of the most prominent features of living in the twenty-first century. Especially since the coronavirus pandemic, we've felt uncertainty in our lives like never before. The world sometimes feels like it's spiraling into oblivion, and it's not clear what we can do on an individual or corporate level to stop it. Uncertainty is not a new phenomenon, but we have more information about what's going on in the world than we ever have before. We know more about what we don't know.

Uncertainty may be a hallmark of modern existence, but it's the bane of every corporate decision maker. This is why so much of business school focuses on closing the uncertainty gap, rather than managing uncertainty. That's a mistake—not because we shouldn't try to find the right kinds of data to help us make decisions, but because it sets up the false impression that the world is thoroughly knowable. Instead of preparing leaders of tomorrow to make fast-moving decisions with imperfect information, schools are shifting their focus to competencies in data analytics, providing even more security blankets against uncertainty. Better data is a good thing; better analysis is even more helpful. But the world is too complex to eliminate uncertainty altogether.

Technical uncertainty is a particularly insidious part of modern management. We've talked at length about why it's so hard to navigate change in a digital world, but part of the problem is that our technical debt (the dependent systems and code we've built over time that have grown like weeds) makes changing directions hard, and uncertainty about the direction of technical progress makes knowing what direction to change in even harder. The combination leads organizations to either decision paralysis, or an exceeding commitment to one strategic direction (such as a large-scale system implementation already in progress) even after we have better information.

The best defense against uncertainty is a good offense. What we should be doing is helping leaders unsure about their knowledge gaps manage investment decisions across multiple time horizons, and empowering them with skills for adaptive change management. We've talked a lot already about adaptive change management, so let's focus on investment decisions. At 18 Coffees, we've encouraged clients to think about investments across three time horizons using a 70/20/10 model of investment.

Investment Model

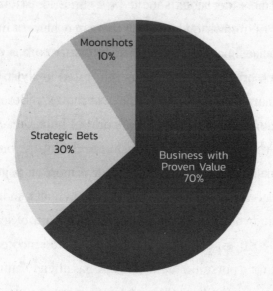

Moonshots
10%

Strategic Bets
30%

Business with
Proven Value
70%

You should put 70 percent of your investment (including time, talent, and money) into the activities you're most sure have value. These are often defensive maneuvers, spending money to double down on areas of the business you already know are working, shoring up areas of competitive advantage. But that 70 percent can also represent parts of the business that you know have a limited lifespan, where you can see new disruptors moving into the marketplace.

Of the remaining 30 percent, 20 percent should be going to strategic bets you're making on new lines of business, innovations in your business model, or other investments that you have relative assurance will pay off. You've done your research, you have at least some available data that tell you this is the right direction for the future of your business.

The last 10 percent is the trickiest because it represents operating with the most uncertainty. But approximately 10 percent of your investment decisions should be aiming for strategic moonshots, areas of innovation for which there may be very limited data. This investment may be the hardest to justify to board members, shareholders, or other stakeholders interested in short-term financial performance, but it's one of the best moves a leader can make to guard against uncertainty. In a world of imperfect data, smart leaders use their imagination to push into the future, but they have to have some flexibility to make their ideas more than just ideas.

One successful company that famously puts money behind moonshot innovations is Alphabet, parent company of search engine Google. In 2010, Google famously spun out X, a moonshot factory dedicated to the pursuit of wild ideas. X has already launched products that were famous flops (Google Glass, for one) and have been the butt of jokes about the tech industry on the satire TV show *Silicon Valley*. But the company's dedication to X and other moonshot businesses is relentless in the face of quarterly pressure from Wall Street, incurring billions of dollars in losses every quarter. Notably, the company also creates space for 20 percent of its employees' schedules to be dedicated to working on projects that may have no promise of an immediate payoff, a famous policy called 20 percent time.

Setting aside some investment outside of normal day-to-day operations is not only a smart business decision, but it's also crucial to maintaining competitive advantage in a world where disruptors can come out of nowhere. But sometimes innovative ideas can be right under our noses, and if we're paying close enough attention, we can get our investment ideas from the unexpected interplay between people and teams, or the unexpected uses of our products by consumers. These kinds of emergent data happen when individual parts of a system interact in ways we didn't expect, leading to behaviors that are native only to the system itself. New opportunities for innovation arise if we're paying attention to them. Emergence is a key concept in complexity and systems theory because of its prominence and observable nature.

The longer out on the timeline we look, the more likely we are to notice and encounter emergence and uncertainty. They point to ambiguity as a key element of complexity, and, unfortunately, mean that we as leaders have to become more comfortable with living in a world that is black, white, and gray all at the same time. But I believe within this ambiguity there can be beauty as well.

One emergent property endemic to nature that I believe has implications for how we think about business scale is called stochastic self-similarity, the tendency of some systems to statistically mimic themselves at various scales out of seeming chaos. Forests mimic the same patterns as the leaves on a tree, and coastlines show the same properties as grains of sand. The fractals of snowflakes are maybe the most famous example of nature's self-similarity. If we look hard enough, I believe we can use the model of nature to find scalable solutions to our most pressing problems. All it takes is the right level of magnification.

You Are a Complicated Mess

We've covered a number of logical fallacies and cognitive biases throughout this book as we've explored what makes change hard in organizations. Suffice it to say, we've only scratched the surface of what makes working with fallible humans like us hard. We are complexities in ourselves, systems built on our past experiences (imperfect data, at best) that interpret the world with more emotion than logic. Put a bunch of us together trying to solve an intractable systemic problem, and it's no wonder so many change initiatives fail.

One of the most common ways I've seen human behavior sabotage organizations is through the misalignment of expectations. How many meetings have you come out of thinking your team decided to do one thing, only to have someone else hear that you decided to do another? There are mitigations, of course, including making sure someone is taking notes and capturing action items and who's responsible for them as they're discussed (highly recommended, if you're not already doing this), but every organization is constantly fighting to keep everyone on the same page.

Problems with managing expectations aren't just part of meetings and workstreams, either. A few years ago, right as the pandemic hit, one of my clients found that the new world of remote work was going better than anyone had expected, except that the tension between the more senior leaders on some teams and the younger, more remote-flexible junior-level employees was reaching a boiling point. After some investigation, we found that the senior managers, most of whom had families with kids stuck home doing remote school, were exhibiting some bitterness about the globetrotting being undertaken by some of the younger employees, who saw the move to remote work as a chance to abandon their small city apartments and do some traveling. Performance numbers had not suffered. The company also had no stated policy against flexing one's remote work location, and the managers had never communicated their expectations that the individual contributors stay home. The feedback came under the guise of professionalism: "I wish Alex would be more professional on calls with potential clients. He seems to be in a new place every other week."

Generational and cultural diversity can be an organizational strength, but it is also one of the biggest contributors to misaligned expectations. Our employees come from different assumptions about how the world works, different families of origin who instilled different values. In the workplace, those cultural expectations often collide. Many studies have shown how cultural diversity leads to better business outcomes because the company benefits from different viewpoints and ideas, but often companies struggle to truly take advantage of the diversity they have by focusing on including the right voices when it matters. Instead of intentional inclusion, the unstated expectation is often that other cultures have to fall in line with the one that dominates the workplace.

Miscommunication is a common part of any workplace experience even without unstated expectations. We are constantly interpreting, reinterpreting, and misinterpreting each other's intentions—and that dynamic is made more acute when we throw remote work into the mix and lose much of the body language we depend on to help us understand and interpret communication. Nonverbal communication has been said to be somewhere between 70 and 90 percent of all communication, and yet we're reduced to interpreting it through tiny, *Brady Bunch*-like 2D windows. Even if we remove our tendency to interpret the world through cognitive fallacies and assume that the information we get from each other is perfectly rational, *perfectly rational* doesn't necessarily mean understood.

These are some of the individual human dynamics that contribute to complexity, but group human behavior is also an important culprit. In groups, our fallacies turn into collective neuroses, and our rational thinking becomes overridden by our desire not to upset the group dynamics. I've seen this play out in boardrooms where important decisions were being made. I was once working with a major consumer brand, making important decisions about an expensive ad campaign. When the creative treatment crafted by the advertising agency was shown, it was clear it could be offensive to a certain subset of the population. But it was fun, and the brand director was sold on the idea. I spoke up against the ad, cautioning that it could lead to an internet backlash. But no one else in the room wanted to row against the tide. Everyone was experiencing the good feelings of having made a decision. The ad ran, and the predicted backlash happened. A few weeks later, I was counseling the same brand director on damage control.

As we zoom out from individual behavior to our organization as a whole, complexity becomes an easier concept to understand because we begin to see our organization as a fallible system that also happens to be made of fallible component parts. One person leaving their job, for example, may be a rational decision based on their own needs. Maybe their career isn't advancing, their job isn't fulfilling, or they're seeking higher pay. But start to scale out that behavior, with others making the same decision at the same time, and suddenly the organization has a crisis on its hands, and leaders have to make a decision based not on one person's rationality but on the herd behavior of a group of people seeing each other make decisions to exit. Zoom out again, and cultural phenomena like the 2021 Great Resignation, when massive numbers of employees left their jobs, become apparent.

Human dynamics are an essential part of understanding complexity, but they don't have to slow down innovation or hinder the process of managing change. With some intentional interventions, we can surface unstated expectations, map the cultures of our workplaces, and truly take advantage of the wonders of different kinds of people working together toward a common goal. Some of the interventions we have suggested to clients aren't new or innovative but part of management best practices, such as having effective one-on-ones and leaving room for the right voices in group meetings. These kinds of best practices can't be understated as important. But some new types of employee engagement opportunities present ways to use new digital tools to acknowledge and manage complexity in the employee experience.

Consistent communication should be a paramount objective for any organization but especially during a time of change. Using techniques we perfected in Obama political organizing, the 18 Coffees team has worked with companies to broaden how they think about internal communication and employee motivation, using a combination of email, text messaging, and occasional internal messages on apps or company message boards to reinforce the vision for change and maximize clarity. We'll never be able to completely mitigate employee confusion or turn complexity into perfect clarity. But by organizing ourselves and our company around an effective employee experience at both the individual and corporate level, we can at least mitigate complexity's most damaging effects.

Toward Learning Organizations

What is the cure for living in a complex world? There is no panacea, but one approach that makes organizations more adaptable, and therefore gives organizations more opportunities for ethical behavior, is to create an environment of constant learning. Some call it the practice of knowledge management, but I think that's a misnomer. Knowledge isn't an element of complexity unleashed upon the world that has to be controlled; it's something buried within complex systems that has to be mined. Complex systems are already learning and relearning, and there are new opportunities to gain knowledge within our organizations all the time if we can tap into that learning process. We call this the practice of recursive learning.

Recursive learning is the constant review of core assumptions, the analysis of new emergent data, and the reapplication of strategy. It's not just about us learning as individuals within a system—though that is also important as component parts of that system—it's about us acknowledging that effective organizations are those that are able to mine insights from complex operations. If emergent data arises from unexpected interactions within our company's walls, how do we intentionally mine that data for new insights?

The story of the creation of Moderna's mRNA COVID-19 vaccine is a fascinating recent example of emergence that led to a breakthrough innovation. Moderna emerged out of Flagship Pioneering, a life sciences venture firm, and since its conception, it has been dedicated to the research and application of mRNA molecules. (The name *ModeRNA* hints at its mission.)

The road to a vaccine was never guaranteed. Scientists at Flagship and eventually Moderna experimented with using mRNA in several different capacities, building on several different technologies over many years before landing on the creation of biotherapeutic drugs and eventually vaccines. The team used a technique of consistent learning, mining emergent data, and reapplying what they were learning to new theories.

Scientific breakthroughs have always thrived on this kind of recursive learning. What would happen if all of our organizations approached problem-solving with the same level of curiosity? Instead, I've often seen clients only look for the data points that reinforce the current strategy and validate their current assumptions. The best use of recursive learning always leaves room for the unexpected.

One client of mine, a global advertising and PR agency, demonstrated a fantastic use of recursive learning. Instead of limiting knowledge sharing to case studies presented after one of their client's campaigns ended, the agency created several touchpoints for learning along the way as different teams were working on different client accounts. The initiative had four fronts: an internal messaging forum shared by all employees with pre-seeded discussions meant to surface insights about how each account was functioning, time set aside during one-on-one management meetings dedicated to what each employee was learning, in-person events open to the entire agency with rapid-fire presentations given by team members about successful ideas (and, importantly, unsuccessful ideas) they had on one account that could apply to others, and time given during all-hands meetings to talk about some of the most innovative learnings across the organization. With this comprehensive approach, the agency was able to close the knowledge gap between teams and rapidly innovate on behalf of their clients.

An enterprise's ability to continually reorganize itself in the face of new data is a survival tactic in the face of a constantly changing market. But it's also an imperative for any enterprise looking to live its values. That kind of adaptive skill allows an enterprise to acknowledge areas of ethical lapse, and, importantly, to reorganize itself to do better. Recursive learning allows us to acknowledge that we never truly know what the consequences of our actions may be.

We never see the world with perfect vision or understanding, and we should be highly skeptical of any business leader, politician, or (I'm sorry to say) consultant who claims that they can. We have to operate our organizations with radical self-awareness and honesty, and whenever we think we have something—a framework, a process, a strategy—completely figured out, periodically take a look at it with fresh eyes. The only way to begin operating ethically in a complex world is not only to learn and learn again, but also to apply those new learnings to how we operate (the Angelouian principle).

Leaning into Ambiguity

A cornerstone of modernity has been the pursuit of certainty, and when we're not certain, conforming reality to the demands of our certainty rather than living with any uncertainty. Growing up in a conservative culture and then going into progressive politics taught me that people are willing to see only the data points that conform to their preexisting point of view. I even fell into this trap, in both directions, willing to demonize the "godless liberals destroying family life" before I raged against the "gun-toting bigots holding back progress." The desire for certainty is a social pathosis as much as a personal one.

In Simone de Beauvoir's seminal work *The Ethics of Ambiguity*, the feminist and philosopher points to how modern life is filled with tension. We are individuals with our own desires and internal complexities who find ourselves a part of governments, companies, and other collective systems. We are subjects who make individual moral decisions every day on the objects of our actions, but we are also objects influenced by subjective systems. We are an amalgamation of our past experiences and yet have agency over our future decisions. We are an approximation of our situational circumstances, but with the will to act, we can transcend them.

Many modern thinkers point to one side or the other of each of these dualities as an answer to why we feel so restless about life, but Beauvoir argues that ambiguity is an essential part of existence. If we feel tension, it's because we're meant to feel it. Instead of running away from it, we should lean into it, become familiar with the unease, get comfortable. In fact, she argues that we should be skeptical of anyone who offers easy answers to life's hardest problems.

This thinking is hard for executives to reconcile with many of the diagnostic solutions we are offered in business school. Good strategy, we are taught, is about finding the "right" answer to any given market-based situation at any given time. This is why executives have fallen head over heels in love with data in the past decade: it provides a comfort blanket against ambiguity. But if ambiguity is a defining feature of modern life, it's certainly also one in a fast-moving business environment. Many consultants have tried to update strategic models to take into account shifting business dynamics, and some of them have some practical validity. But no consultant worth their salt will admit to the level of ambiguity in decision-making Beauvoir claims. (If they did, they'd probably be out of a job.)

Personally, I think living in ambiguity and complexity is extremely hard—so much so that we seek out certainty wherever we can find it. We hire consultants, go to conferences, apply new models and frameworks, and read new books (yes, even this one) all to find some new truth about how the world works and to pursue closing the ambiguity gap and convince ourselves of the right decisions. As we'll see in the next chapter, creating a north star for yourself can help close some of this ambiguity gap because it helps create meaning for yourself and your company out of a seemingly ambiguous world.

9

Find Your Center of Gravity

When 18 Coffees was founded, there was no guarantee we'd be where we are today, or even that we'd build the kind of company we are. My cofounder, business partner, and longtime confidant Robin Chung and I knew that we wanted to venture out on our own. We had the entrepreneurial bug and the conviction that we could do what we do better than anyone else. But we needed the *why*. Beyond the potential income, beyond the freedom that running your own company provides (which, spoiler alert, also comes with massive anxiety), we both needed something baked into our work that was about making a difference. We'd given our labor to other people for decades for what often felt like banal work, sometimes bordering on socially detrimental. How was our company going to be any different?

In a series of intense one-on-one meetings—yes, over lots of coffee—Robin and I worked through the answer together. We both came from a digital strategy background, and we knew the implications of digital on business better than anyone. We also knew that most business leaders underestimated the social implications of the new digital environment and how empowered consumers were shifting expectations for business leaders, wanting them to be moral leaders as well. And we knew from painful personal experience that most large enterprises were not prepared to operate in this new hyper-connected, radically conscious environment. So we focused on building a consulting firm operating at the intersection of digital transformation, social change, and the future of work.

From the beginning, we said not only would that focus shape the kinds of services and products we would offer, but if we were going to ask our clients to think critically about those issues, we needed to do it for ourselves as well. We had to hold ourselves to an even higher standard, thinking critically about how we operated our own business, about how our own company leaned into social issues and used digital tools. That strategic focus shaped our values, those values shaped our operating principles, and as we've grown, we've come back to that thinking repeatedly as a north star for who we are and why we exist.

Navigating the business of making change in our radically conscious environment is tough work, but it's made tougher by not actually knowing where you're going. There may be no point B on our journey toward better, but we still have to be pointed in a direction. Otherwise we risk getting lost in a number of infinite possibilities, infinite interpretations of what *better* could mean for ourselves and our business.

Leading change means finding moments to strategically create conflict, whether that's internally within people who need to see a problem differently, within an enterprise that could use a good cleansing fire, or even as a representative of that enterprise within society. We need more leaders willing to step up and speak out on behalf of the parts of society that need changing, who feel comfortable enough pushing for better in the uncomfortable position of not having all the answers yet.

When faced with change, we often react by asking for perfect information, but change never happens that way. Leaders are always balancing ambiguity with the urgency to act now. Having a sense of direction can help create boundaries around the uncomfortable tension of wanting better but not being there yet.

Three things really matter for finding some kind of north star that can help guide your people forward: leadership, ethical guideposts, and a process for adjudication of differences.

The Two Dimensions of Leadership

Your role as a leader—of a company, a community, a family, whatever it may be—is to strategically create chaos in order to orchestrate the kind of regeneration your enterprise needs. We've already talked about how leadership is about empowering people to make the kind of change they want to see. Sometimes there is something broken underneath the surface and everyone knows it, but no one has the courage to step up and organize people to fix it. Real leaders seize the opportunity to be a catalyst.

Management is what keeps the chaos in check. If leaders create chaos through the strategic deployment of dissonance, managers reduce it through weaving disparate chaotic themes back together into a cohesive whole. Leaders tap into the emotional core of an organization, whereas managers have to look beyond the emotion to see a situation as it actually is and manage the technical details. Organizations need both, and it is hard, but not impossible, for someone to be naturally skilled at both. Since *leader* is a sexy term that everyone aspires to, whereas *manager* carries with it some bureaucratic implications, I like to call this the two dimensions of leadership. Self-awareness involves asking yourself where your natural skills lie, and, depending on your situation, either supplementing the skills you lack with another person with those strengths, or training yourself to play both roles as much as you possibly can.

18 Coffees has benefited from the natural partnership I have with Robin, who is a skilled manager. I am proficient at strategy and naturally futuristic, which makes me a great asset to the company for seeing around corners and knowing where we should head. But I'm terrible with the present details when my head is always in the future. Robin excels at seeing all the aspects of our company right now and understanding the implications for strategy on our teams and clients. She's also incredibly intuitive about how our teams and clients are feeling, whereas I can get so lost in my head about big ideas I lose the thread of taking care of people. We are classically bottom-line versus top-line thinkers, and that tension can often put us in conflict. But the tension is also what makes us function as effective leaders of our company. When our staff knows we've come to a decision, they know it has been debated by the two of us and sharpened by each other's thinking.

I've seen managers who've struggled with not having one or the other dimension of leadership, and watched their staff get frustrated by either the lack of details and direction, or the obsession with tasks at the expense of the bigger picture. Smart leaders recognize their deficits and supplement their skills, sometimes with training, sometimes by delegating to members of their team who have skills they, the leaders, lack. And sometimes they can add particular workflows that help. One natural manager I know puts time on his calendar every week to make sure he's stepping back from the everyday work to reflect on the bigger picture.

Applying the two dimensions of leadership is important when leading an organization through a large-scale change because employees need both excitement about the bigger picture and assurance that the details will be taken into consideration. Creating strategic chaos is an important part of making change, but managing that discomfort, making sure that a team can hold itself in the tension of ambiguity without disengaging or devolving, is just as important.

How Ethical Guideposts Support Values

There are movable parts of an organization, and then there are supposedly immovable parts. Mission and vision statements, for example, are things we put on paper that are supposed to stand the test of time, things that guide operational decisions day-to-day that rarely get revisited. But mission and vision statements are often idealized notions of our operations that don't take into account the kinds of ethical quandaries we often find ourselves in while doing business in complex environments.

Values statements are a good start and are often (but not always) developed along with an organizational mission and vision.

Values statements begin to moralize not just what a company does or what it stands for, but also how it will act and how it expects its employees to act. This behavioral focus helps create guidelines for operations when situations get sticky or hard decisions need to be made, but values statements are often so generic that they open themselves up to wide interpretation upon application. It's great that a company says it values authenticity and inclusivity, but how does that help a program manager know whether or not the exclusion of a particular audience from a product rollout is good business practice or harmful to a specific marginalized community? How does it help a user-experience designer know whether or not a particular user flow is encouraging or addicting? Employees need more specific guidance about the application of a company's values in particular situations.

At 18 Coffees, we've started digging deeper on values statements by working with teams to create ethical guideposts that are meant to help bring a company's values into practical application. By exploring specific ethical situations and forcing some hard questions internally before they're forced upon the organization by external forces, we've been able to put on paper more boundaries that define what a company will and will not do in specific situations. The ambiguity of most values statements can be paralyzing. Managers find the kind of clarity found in ethical guideposts incredibly empowering.

For one of our clients, a major telecommunications company, creating ethical guideposts has been an essential part of launching a new product ethics practice. In coordination with the product, technology, and design teams, 18 Coffees has been working to build a new practice dedicated to the application of product ethics to every new digital and physical product—no small task, considering the company brings hundreds of new products to market every year and makes continual updates to the rest of its product suite on a rolling basis. The creation of ethical guideposts served as the cornerstone of our new strategy for bringing products to market. The process of creating them became a way to include stakeholders throughout the product development process and create ownership and excitement over the new direction.

The process of creating ethical guideposts looks different for every organization, but doing it properly always involves a few key steps, outlined in the list that follows. First, it's important to get the right stakeholders involved in the process early on. The development of guidelines that will directly affect the day-to-day work—especially ones involving ethical issues that are easily confused and can be hotly debated—needs the direct involvement of the people who'll be affected by them. And depending on the issues being debated, it also often needs the voices of marginalized employees or customers. Senior executives in the company who have decision-making power over the work are also an important audience because they will ultimately be able to determine the success of the implementation.

Perspectives from these audiences need to be collected and considered, though not every perspective should necessarily carry equal weight. Using qualitative methods (such as interviews and focus groups) and quantitative methods (such as surveys), the goal is to understand where the organization may have some ethical dissonance about the issues it is facing. For example, do employees always agree that inclusivity should be considered when developing target market criteria? Are there limits, and if so where do they exist? Knowing where further exploration will be necessary before a consensus is reached is important.

Ethical Guidepost Action Steps
1. Involve the right stakeholders early.
2. Consider which voices are not represented.
3. Decide on ethical boundaries and nonstarters.
4. Create opportunity for collaboration and consensus.
5. Draft, revise, and approve language.
6. Merchandise and celebrate the new guideposts.
7. Revisit and revise at regular intervals.

And finally, the process of drafting, revising, and approving the language of the guideposts is an important consideration. Depending on the size of the organization, we often start with a workshop highlighting the results of our discovery research and allow different team members to weigh in on language they'd like to see included. But then a smaller team will put language on paper and work to finalize the guideposts, getting approval and sponsorship from the senior leaders whose teams will be involved.

Ethical guideposts are meant to become woven into the fabric of the immovable part of the organization, but as we've already covered, even the most thorough and well-established guideposts will need revisiting at certain intervals. Emergent data can help provide clarity on whether our guideposts were thorough enough or whether they created any unintended consequences. And even when the guideposts still serve us well, they will never anticipate every situation. As we'll cover later in this chapter, we still need a process for adjudicating situations that fall between the cracks of our expectations.

Finding Solid Philosophical Ground

I've seen the creation of ethical guideposts work for several organizations, but it takes some preparation. As much as our business environment has started having conversations about "business for good," and as much as we have started talking about being socially conscious and living our values as individuals, we still have no shared definition of what living our values actually means. There is no philosophical grounding for how to create ethical guideposts without forcing some conversations around what *the right thing to do* means.

Perhaps it would help if we first delineated between what *morals* and *ethics* mean, words I've seen used interchangeably within organizations. *Ethics* can be defined as set of rules or recognized behavior as it relates to moral principles but codified into a system of moral behavior, often quite formally in certain professional situations (think of the Hippocratic oath for medical professionals). *Morals* are an individual's standards for right or wrong behavior, often informed by some kind of ethical framework within which they are operating. So being immoral and being unethical are actually two different things, and—stay with me—it's actually possible to be one and not be the other. It helps to have some basic understanding of some of the major Western schools of thought around ethics and how they can apply in different business environments. Let's explore three here.

The first is called virtue ethics and can be traced back to ancient Greek philosophers like Socrates. Virtue ethics holds concepts of moral virtue (courage, modesty, temperance) as central to ethical foundations. For organizations, it focuses on the virtuous behavior of employees individually as crucial to the organization behaving ethically as a collective. Companies may have values statements that form the basis of expectations of individual behavior, but organizations that operate with a strong focus on virtue ethics will also thoroughly consider the virtue of the person they are hiring as representative of their organization. Ethical guideposts with virtues at their core will frame up individual moral behavior as key, asking questions like, "Does this decision line up with how we value inclusivity? If I make this decision, am I modeling inclusivity as an employee?"

Like all philosophical groundwork, virtue ethics is not without its criticisms, and maybe the most substantial for virtue ethics is that it can be seen as culturally relative. Different societies will have different viewpoints on what constitutes a virtue, so grounding an organization in a culturally specific virtue gives the organization only a culturally specific ethical footing. Another criticism is that virtue ethics does not focus enough on delineating what actions are permissible, and opens up the organization to too much subjective interpretation of the application of a virtue.

Deontology, or duty ethics, is a branch of ethics that concerns itself with what the right thing to do in any given situation is. Unlike virtue ethics, deontology is concerned with the morality of each action by an employee and the intentions of the employee when carrying out that action. Moral obligations can be defined in ethical guideposts by the organization but often are also informed by external sources such as the religious or political beliefs of the employee. Importantly, ethics concerned with duty holds that there are some choices that cannot be justified by what outcomes they bring about no matter how good (even morally good) those outcomes may be. Ethical guideposts based on duty will always be more concerned with the right than the good.

Critiques of deontological thinking mostly come from the third school of thought I want to explore: consequentialism, or the idea that the only true way to judge the morality of an action is by the consequences of that action. A morally right act (or absence of acting) from a consequentialist standpoint is one that produces the morally right outcome. Ethical guideposts created with consequentialist leanings are typically future facing and concerned about market impacts, utilitarian in their concern for what the organizational machine is producing and how it affects customers, users, communities, and audiences. Unlike deontology, which is about doing the right thing in spite of the outcome, consequentialists believe, famously, that the ends justify the means.

Understanding the impacts on customers, users, communities, or audiences sounds good in theory, but in practice it is very hard. For one, the consequences for various stakeholders may be at odds, for example, creating economic hardship for one subset of customers at the expense of supporting another.

Consequentialism takes a kind of moral imagination of the highest order and suffers from what critics call the ideal observer problem. It depends on an omniscient observer who is able to grasp all the consequences of any given action. Individual actors such as employees are always operating with less than perfect information and have no way of understanding all the possible consequences of their actions. As was pointed out in *The Good Place*, basing an ethical theory on outcomes alone is hard in an interconnected world of unintended consequences.

No ethical philosophy is perfect, and all of the above approaches have been debated and redebated for centuries. Only in the recent era of modern business has ethics started to be applied to management theories, and the marriage of moral theory with studies in behavioral economics has brought up interesting dilemmas in regard to organizational ethical behavior. Suffice it to say, every organization has to decide for itself what its ethical guideposts will be and which application of what ethical theory it will apply in what situations. And, importantly, it's up to the right kinds of leaders to create space (and strategic chaos) to have these kinds of hard conversations.

Adjudicating Differences

The best ethical frameworks have holes, and the best ethical guideposts won't anticipate every situation. So how do organizations that want to do better navigate unanticipated situations?

An engagement with companies to implement ethical guideposts involves doing the hard work of transforming business practice around those guideposts and changing team behavior to match the new ethically driven strategy. But our next step is typically to develop collaboratively an adjudication approach for reconciling ethically sticky situations. Putting an adjudication process in place typically looks like developing an ethics review board composed of internal and external stakeholders who can make decisions that then serve as "case law" internally and inform other decisions down the road.

Case law is a helpful metaphor here because of how legal cases are customarily adjudicated. In the US, how a judge construes the law is typically divided into several kinds of interpretations. Statutory law is based on legislation, and regulatory law is established by executive agencies. But case law is law based on precedent, when a judge considers the rulings of other courts as an important part of their ruling. This is why attorneys arguing cases will cite other specific cases, especially those that went before the Supreme Court, as evidence of precedent.

In the context of a business, regulation and statute have typically been the domain of compliance and HR, and have been driven by outside forces that govern the behavior of an organization based on how society deems it should behave. But organizations doing the hard work of aiming for better don't want to aim for compliance alone. They want to hold themselves to a higher standard. Hence the creation of ethical guideposts and the need for ethical leadership. And just as compliance interprets regulations and determines the approach the company should take to be within them, adherence to ethical guideposts has to be situationally determined.

Creating an ethics review board is one way we've helped organizations adhere to their own ethical standards. The review board is typically comprised of internal stakeholders—sometimes even ethicists who have been hired directly by the company to advise on day-to-day operations—and external consultants who help give the company an unbiased perspective. The review board analyzes escalated issues within the company when there is a measure of internal debate, whether because the ethical guideposts provide room for interpretation regarding an issue, or because they don't clearly address it at all. The structure of the board depends on the size and scope of the enterprise's operations, but, importantly, its decisions have to be seen as final. Executive leadership can't have leeway to overrule.

Once the board has been convened, the process and procedures have been established, and it starts making rulings on cases brought before it, those rulings become part of the case law of ethical understanding for the organization and start filling any gaps in understanding that the ethical guideposts don't address. Until those guideposts are revisited, the guideposts themselves, the adjudicated cases, and the ongoing cases are what determine the boundaries of the company's operations and help the company remain agile while having some confidence about its ethical footing.

An ethical review board is one way to help a company live up to its stated guidelines. We've also helped companies that are specifically concerned about their impact in marginalized communities create community review boards made up of representatives from those communities. Similarly, the review boards are composed of both internal and external representatives, but unlike ethics review boards, only issues that will have the potential to impact the community will be escalated to community review boards.

These types of governance approaches work only in conjunction with the designing and implementation of ethical guideposts because that process forces conversations about what a company will or won't do in most situations. Implementing an ethics board without it is a recipe for confusion and frustration on behalf of employees, and is a lot of wasted time by the board. But when this process works like it's supposed to work, a company can continue to move swiftly, be competitive, and have some assurance that it is still operating in a manner that is consistent with the values of its leadership, its employees, its shareholders, and all of its other stakeholders.

Toward Better in Business and Society

Forming ethical guideposts is a great strategy for steering an organization through change if you know what you want those guideposts to be. I'm generally agnostic when I work with clients about how they create their guideposts and what ethical frameworks they rely on to formulate them. After all, philosophers have debated ethics for centuries for a reason. There is no one right answer. But I do have opinions about what we should all be aiming for as we create more ethical and inclusive organizations.

To reference Beauvoir again, a pioneer in existentialist thought, we are born free to make our own choices, but we are "condemned" (as her partner, Jean-Paul Sartre, famously put it) to always bear the responsibility of those choices and their consequences. It's so important to understand how complex the world actually is because unintended consequences are abundant. We should always be skeptical of people who believe they see the world with perfect moral clarity and objectivity or who think they can remove themselves from their own bias. We can never fully remove ourselves from our own experiences and how they have colored our perception of the world, but we can be aware of them and honest about them.

So if we live in a world where we are free to make our own choices and suffer the consequences, what does that mean for how we live together in that world? Beauvoir believed we should aim for an ethics that maximizes that freedom for everyone, giving everyone the same kind of ability to make their own choices, and that we should be honest about the fact that we live in a society where that kind of freedom is not equally distributed. Our freedom is contingent on how others have willed it into being in the past; our meaning is determined by our relationships with others. Because our freedom is so dependent on other people, Beauvoir believed that we have a moral obligation to will the freedom of others, to work to dismantle systems of oppression. An ethics that maximizes personal freedom can't exclude the intersectionality of the freedom of those around us.

In a business environment, I believe this means recognizing the ways in which our business has become a part of systems of oppression and actively working to dismantle them, sometimes at the expense of more profits. It means going beyond creating moral employees, recognizing that individual moral behavior doesn't operate in a vacuum. And it means digging in on anti-oppression work of all kinds, including but not exclusive to race, gender, age, and sexual identity.

The United Nations Guiding Principles on Business and Human Rights (UNGPs) have been a good starting place for several enterprises, and the reporting framework has been adopted by companies like Unilever, Ericsson, and Nestlé. The principles attempt to put in place a global standard for businesses endeavoring to address adverse impacts on human rights related to their business activity, including mitigating impacts by their business relationships and supply chain. Tying the creation of an ethical north star to the UNGPs gives large enterprises an easily accessible framework as a starting point.

Beyond looking at our own company's operations, I also believe the work of maximizing freedom and minimizing oppression means directing our companies to actively engage in social life, not to be afraid of getting political. We can never truly be a part of the work of anti-oppression by only navel-gazing about what's happening within our walls. It's not about politics; it's about principles.

We have to remember that what is considered political and what is not is a social construct and often changes. Target did not consider its bathrooms political until it made the decision in 2016 to be transgender inclusive, allowing customers and employees to use the bathroom that corresponded with their gender identity. The subsequent conservative backlash placed the retailer at the center of a national dialogue about transgender identity, immediately politicizing what could have been a routine corporate decision. Companies that let the fear of becoming political drive their decisions are at risk of being thrust into political debates anyway, without any of the moral authority they would have earned by taking a stand when it is politically risky to do so.

I've thought a lot about the best way to direct change in large, complex organizations over the past decade, and I've come to the conclusion that when change is about both improving the organization and making it a better corporate citizen, there is a better chance of success. Employees want causes they can believe in, and given the opportunity I've seen them time and again rally around a chance to take pride in how their workplace operates in the world. Being a part of a large enterprise can sometimes feel like getting caught in the machine of exploitative capitalism with no recourse. The chance to turn that machine into a force for good, even by degrees, can be a motivating factor in employee retention and a success factor for any change initiative.

A Kind of Disruption Worth Fighting For

Whose responsibility is it to make your city, your community, your company better? Whether or not you realize it, you've been selected by history to be an empowered leader. Making change is now your responsibility.

We are at a serious crossroads as a global community. As technology has enabled us to be more connected and mobile, misinformation and disinformation by bad actors have threatened our ability to function in democratic ways. As climate change becomes more a centerpiece of global policy, optimism around solving it has been hard to find even as new innovations in carbon capture are starting to be funded and scaled. And as the wealthy parts of the world start to emerge from a global pandemic, concern is rising for how the virus will be contained in regions that still have no access to abundant vaccines. It is extremely easy to become paralyzed and cynical in the face of the kinds of problems that are ahead of us. But you have more power to make change than you even realize, and your sphere of influence is greater than you see when you're caught up in the everyday.

Turning your company into a more ethical organization, making it less exploitative by what may feel like imperceptible degrees, may seem trivial in the face of the kinds of large, complex problems we're facing. But we're going to have to build the new radically conscious economy one organization at a time. If you believe, as I do, that business can be a force for good, that we're not fated for endless exploitative capitalism, then we're going to have to make change collectively—and it's not always going to feel like it's moving quickly enough. In fact, change will probably always feel like it's coming too slowly.

But you and I have a responsibility to act. It doesn't matter what your title is or what position you hold or don't hold in your community. You have been given more power, more information than any of your historical predecessors by nature of the supercomputer you carry around in your pocket. With that power comes a responsibility to act, and I believe abdicating that responsibility is a decision none of us should take lightly. You are a part of history unfolding, which makes you at least partially responsible for how it unfolds.

When I was feeling lost and a bit desperate for clarity after the 2016 US election, I encountered many friends and family members who felt the same. But unlike me, they hadn't worked in politics or advocacy before and didn't have the tools for how to focus their newfound anger into something positive. So I created a worksheet I called the personal impact canvas to help them focus on making change without getting lost in the bottomless number of

Ambition

How do you want to change the world?

Assets	Issues you care about			Constraints
What do you bring to the table that's unique to you?	What keeps you up at night?			What non-negotiables do you have?

Time Horizons →

	Now (In the next year)	The short term (1–5 years)	The long term (5+ years)
Areas of influence → How will you fulfill your ambition?			
You			
Your social circle			
Your world			

Growth Opportunities

Your Impact

What new things do you need to make your ambition possible?

This personal impact canvas was made by Caleb Gardner. Feel free to use and adapt it however it'll help you change the world. (But please don't try to sell it.)
Go to https://calebgardner.com/personal-impact-canvas for a downloadable version.

possibilities for how to use their time, and I gave it away to the public. The canvas became extremely popular and was adapted by several organizations to be used as a facilitated group activity. If you're struggling with understanding your sphere of influence or where to start making change, this tool may help you get started.

The goal is to not become lost in the infinite, paralyzed by problems that feel too big to solve. We have to find our own context again in whatever ways we can.

I've never been more hopeful about our ability to solve what's in front of us, and I believe we all have a part to play in making a better future. There's no point B in sight—change is ongoing, and disruption is inevitable. But if you believe like I do that we'll get the kind of disruption we're willing to fight for, there's no time like the present to start making history.

ACKNOWLEDGMENTS

This book wouldn't have been possible without the tireless effort of my very patient book agent, Susan Raihofer. Thanks for the long hours of helping to refine the idea and turn my very muddled brain into words on paper. Thanks also to Matt Holt, Katie Dickman, and the entire BenBella staff for your work turning this into an amazing final product.

I may have collected the ideas here, but this book is the product of a career supported by many inspiring people over two decades who have mentored me and, at times, taken a chance on me, especially Blagica Bottigliero and Toby Fallsgraff. I'm also grateful to many people who've inspired me, allowed me to bounce ideas off of them, or read words along the way, including but not exclusively Roo Powell, Cassie Marketos, Dave Sandell, Reid Blackman, Vince Brackett, Ian Beacraft, Tracy Goodheart, and Sarah Judd Welch.

The entire 18 Coffees community and the coworkers I get to interact with every day consistently inspire me and challenge my thinking. Special shout-out to my business-partner-in-crime, Robin Chung, for going on this great adventure with me, and consistently tolerating my head being in the clouds. And I'm always grateful to our amazing client partners, alongside whom I get to build things every day.

ACKNOWLEDGMENTS

And finally, I wouldn't have accomplished any of this without my wife, Caroline, who spent countless hours managing our family while I focused on writing. Words can't express the deep appreciation I have for you and for our three children for keeping me grounded and grateful for everyday life.

INDEX

distributed, 170–171, 176
ethical, 172–173
uncertainty and, 186–187
defensive routines, organizational, 121–122
degenerative behavior, 120–125
Delta Airlines, 80–81, 170
democracy
impact of inflammatory content on, 44–45
impact of technology on, 37–38
trust in, 29–30
Democratic National Committee, 37
Democratic Party, 155
Demos, 177
deontology, 208–209
Department of Health and Human Services (DHS), 160
detractors, on change teams, 153
DHL (Dalsey, Hillblom and Lynn), 96
DiCaprio, Leonardo, 3
digital lives, 61–63
digital marketing, 11–14
direction, changes in, 154–155
discipline, public, 64–68
disconnection, social, 23
disruptions, 1–10, 23, 25
distributed decision-making, 170–171, 176
diversity, 191
dogmatism, 18, 57–60, 64–68
Dove, 41–42
dramatic transformation, 31–32
Drucker, Peter, 78
duty ethics (deontology), 208–209

E
Edelman (firm), 11
Edelman Trust Barometer, 29, 169, 178
18 Coffees, 27, 77, 108, 113, 126–127, 132, 136, 155–156, 162, 164, 173, 175, 187, 194, 202, 204
Einstein, Albert, 25
embarrassment, 71–72
emergent data, 183, 189–190, 194–195, 206–207
employees
belief-driven, 178
building brand equity with, 77–79
engagement of, 163
experience of, in work environment, 162–166

frontline, 126, 176
impact of internet on, 52–53
engagement, 73, 80–81, 131–133, 163
Engine No. 1 (hedge fund), 24
Equal Justice Initiative, 177
Ericsson, 215
ESG framework, 7, 82, 177–178
ethical boundaries, 77, 82–83, 206
ethical decision-making, 172–173
ethical guideposts, 201, 203–207
ethics
building brand equity with, 74–82
operationalization of, 49–51
philosophical theories of, 207–210
The Ethics of Ambiguity (Beauvoir), 197
ethics review boards, 211–213
European Union (EU), 47
expectations, misalignment of, 190–191
Expert Political Judgment (Tetlock), 18
external communication, 70–71
Exxon Mobil, 24–25

F
Facebook
addictive user experience of, 49–50
algorithm of, 20, 94
complaints posted on, 73
digital lives on, 61
Dove commercial release on, 41
first-person data collection by, 46
ideological shaming on, 116
insidious online narratives on, 103
misinformation on, 39–40
misuse of, 38
rise of, 12
social consequences on, 81
facts, persuading others with, 54
failure, planning for, 77, 84
false narratives, 101–106
family narrative, in workplace, 166–168
Farren, Meghan, 97
Fauci, Anthony, 17
FBI, 37
FCK campaign, 96–97, 100
feedback loops, 122–123
The Fifth Discipline (Senge), 122
Flagship Pioneering, 195
flexibility, 154–156
Floyd, George, 43, 76, 135, 169
Food Labor Research Center, 78
forecasting, 17–18, 26

January 6, 2021, US Capitol attack, 94, 103, 169
Jobs, Steve, 38
Johnson, Boris, 89
Johnson, Kevin, 177–178
Johnson & Johnson, 149
Journal Business of Ethics, 178
Juno, 35

K
Kahneman, Daniel, 179
Kentucky Fried Chicken (KFC), 96–97
knowledge management, 194

L
ladder of engagement, 131–133
Lawson, Nigel, 137
leadership
  ceding control in, 146
  dimensions of, 201–203
  impact of internet on, 51–56
  impact of social media on, 69–74
  moral, 3–5, 176–178
leading change, 199–219
  adaptive practices for, 175
  by adjudicating differences, 210–213
  by creating strategic chaos, 201–202
  and developing change leaders, 147–150
  dimensions of leadership for, 201–203
  ethical guideposts for, 203–207
  with ethical philosophies, 207–210
  and future shock, 22–28
  by maximizing freedom, 213–216
  in organizations, 147–150
  with personal impact canvasses, 216–219
Lee, Frances S., 59
Lewis, John, 1–2
LinkedIn, 45
listening, 118
Lütke, Tobi, 166–170
Lyft, 130–131

M
Maddow, Rachel, 161
management-centric thinking, 162–163
managers, role of, 149, 153, 201–203
Managing at the Speed of Change (Conner), 143

Massachusetts Institute of Technology (MIT), 115
McDonald's, 179
McKinsey & Company, 126
memories, malleability of, 15–16
Metcalfe, Robert, 20
#MeToo movement, 64, 76
Metro newspaper, 96
microcampaigns, 91
micropersuasion, 54, 90–96
Microsoft, 20, 26
Milner, Ryan, 55
mindset change, 111–134
  coherence and, 117–120
  degenerative behavior and, 120–125
  mission and, 133–134
  rituals for, 111–113, 129–133
  shame and, 113–117
  steps for, 125–129
miscommunication, 192
misinformation, 39, 115
mission-driven adaptability, 159–162, 164–166, 172, 174
mission statements, 133–134, 203
MIT (Massachusetts Institute of Technology), 115
mobile-first mindset, 130–131
Moderna, 195
moonshot projects, 187–188
Moore, Gordon, 20–21
Moore's Law, 20–21
moral entrepreneurship, 176–179
moral leadership, 3–5, 176–178
morals, 207–210
Morin, Edgar, 184–185
Mortal Kombat (video game), 34
Motorola, 124–125
mRNA COVID-19 vaccine, 195
MSL firm, 101
Munoz, Oscar, 72

N
NAACP (National Association for the Advancement of Colored People), 169, 177
naive realism, 87–90, 95–96
Napster, 35
narratives, 85–110
  about climate crisis, 85–87
  for digital platforms, 96–101
  false, 101–106
  family, in work-place, 166–168

227

theory of change, 125–126
3Com, 20
three stories approach, 141–144
TikTok, 99, 101
Time magazine, 16–17
Toffler, Alvin, 23
Tolentino, Jia, 43
transformation, 31–32, 119–120
Trump, Donald, 31, 38–39, 102, 106, 169
trust
   in businesses, 169
   in governments, 29–30, 169
   in media, 169
   in people, 148
truth, misinformation and, 39
twenty-second rule, 131
Twitter, 12, 38, 41, 45, 102, 118
Tyson, Neil deGrasse, 45

U
Uber, 106, 130–131
uncertainty, 185–190
Unilever, 215
United Airlines, 72
United Kingdom, 137
United Nations Guiding Principles
   on Business and Human Rights
   (UNGPs), 214–215
University of California, Berkeley, 78
unrealistic optimism, 16
urban-rural digital divide, 35–36
US government, trust in, 29
US presidential election (2016), 38–40, 217
us-versus them dynamics, 59–60

V
values, public displays of, 63
values statements, 203–204
Vanguard, 24
virtue ethics, 208
vision statements, 203
visual design, for online
   communication, 98

Vivian, C. T., 65, 120
voice, creating company, 98
Vonnegut, Kurt, 99

W
Warby Parker, 171–172
Warzel, Charlie, 44, 66
Watson, Thomas, 20
Wesch, Michael, 62
Westboro Baptist Church, 117–118
WhatsApp, 103
White House, 1–3
White Supremacy in the Age of Trump
   (course), 65
WikiLeaks, 2, 37
Winners Take All (Giridharadas), 169
work environments, 159–179
   adaptive change in, 173–176
   alternatives to hierarchies in, 170–173
   employee experience in, 162–166
   mission-driven adaptability in, 159–162
   moral entrepreneurship in, 176–179
   and workplace teams vs. families, 166–170
work-life boundaries, 164, 168
workplace politics, 141
workplace teams, family narrative
   about, 166–170
workstreams, 174–175
Worn Wear, 75

X
X (moonshot factory), 188–189

Y
YouGov, 97
YouTube, 12

Z
Zipcar, 130–131, 142
Zuboff, Shoshana, 46–47
Zuckerberg, Mark, 38, 40, 46

ABOUT THE AUTHOR

Photo by Toni Graves

Caleb Gardner is an insatiably curious innovation strategist and change management expert who has consulted with startups, global nonprofits, politicians, and Fortune 100 executives to help them navigate disruption and make positive change.

Caleb has developed operational frameworks for a variety of organizations in the public and private sectors, including at professional service firms like Bain & Company and Edelman. For more than three years, Caleb was the lead digital strategist for Organizing for Action (OFA), US President Barack Obama's political advocacy group, running one of the largest digital programs in existence.

Now, as the cofounder and managing partner of 18 Coffees, an innovation and change management firm, Caleb helps train leaders and transform businesses to be more ethical, inclusive, and effective.

Caleb speaks regularly about transformational leadership, managing disruption, and navigating in the new media environment. His keynote presentations have inspired audiences around the globe to understand their capacity to make change.